RPG

also by James McEachin

The Great Canis Lupus
Say Goodnight to the Boys in Blue
The Heroin Factor
Farewell to the Mockingbirds
Tell Me a Tale

James McEachin

Pebbles in the Roadway

Tales and Essays

Bits and Pieces

The Rharl Publishing Group
16161 Ventura Blvd #550, Encino, CA 91436-2523
rharlpublishing.com

Printed and bound in the USA

ISBN 0-965-6661-0-7

1 3 5 7 9 10 8 6 4 2

CIP data available

Pebbles in the Roadway

Ignore nothing on your journey,
Even the pebbles in the roadway.
For there will come a time
When all things change,
And change will be all things.

After the light it became barren. It was vast and still. Primordial, it was. Then it became a landscape of dappled mist that hovered over moorlands of untamed peat bogs and heath. It was timeless, spiritless, as if it were a world without color, shape or meaning. There was no sky, and the air was without movement. Then, from afar, where the horizon should have been, there appeared an almost subversive form that opened the way to a long and winding road that swooped down and wandered into a lifeless oblivion that was surrounded by untold layers of tiny objects. Like pebbles they were. They lay dormant in a void. But then they spoke, first among themselves, then to you, the weary traveler.

They are pebbles, it is confirmed, and it seems now as if they wish to serve as escorts — as companions to you, the traveler, but they remain in place, continuing to talk among themselves, uttering a mixture of languages that can not be entirely heard nor fully understood. It is ever so strange, but you are not troubled. Of late, nothing troubles you, even the mystery of your travels, the alteration of your senses. There is no fear here; there is peace. A blessed peace. You feel that your very soul has been embalmed and is impervious to all things harmful, all things sorrowful. You do not even feel the sadness of those who saw you depart.

When he asked to see you, he described it as his home town. You wondered how that could be. But you left, and now you're here. Judging from what you see, it is nothing in a world of nothingness. But you do not fault him for overstating the case. You merely think of him, and, no longer mindful of the circumstances of your departure, you say to yourself, that's all right; I got your message. I am here, and even though you stretched it, we all are inclined to paint the ol' hometown just a little bit brighter than it actually is. As you consider that bit of logic, your mind, for an instant, shifts back to your hometown. You recall your youth, then bits and pieces of all the years that were to follow your youth. Beady-headed boys are mixed with an array of sights and sounds, distant places and faded faces, and before it is over, all whom you knew and, seemingly, all things that you have known, come to mind. You smile warmly. You move on, again recalling his words.

Your history is his history; your life his life, he said. His words were beyond you then; they are beyond you now. Even more, you still do not remember him. Again you try. Over and over, you try. You try to retrace the voice, trying to attach it to someone — to make it belong to something, but you cannot. You continue to move. Again you cannot help but be taken by the vastness and stillness, and the utterances of the echoing pebbles. They are ceaseless. Then, in a tongue that even you don't understand, you speak — not to them, for they lie behind you now— you are speaking to yourself, asking yourself again and again, What am I doing here? How did I get here? It is ever so strange. But there are no answers. It is perplexing, but not entirely disconcerting. You know the place; but, then again, you do not.

The thought strikes you that perhaps at the start of your journey, you had taken the wrong road; that you had not been on a road at all, and that whatever it was, it has led you astray. You do not belong here, you say again. But, once again, something tells you that you do.

The circumstances of your departure try to nibble through, but they are prevented from doing so. You don't know why; it no longer seems important. You walk on, puzzled.

As it has been from the start, you are without benefit of common sense, but now there is a growing difference. Somehow, you are being imbued with a newness of the senses. It permeates your core. Then, suddenly, you see something up ahead. Other than the pebbled road, you are inclined to believe, it is the first tangible thing you have seen. You are gladdened, but yet you feel no rush from the heart; uplifted, though your being remains aground. Soon you find yourself moving swiftly. You are doing so on legs that are not in motion.

You will not look down again.

Confirmed in your up-ahead view now, is the semblance of a kingdom — or a palace or fiefdom, if you will. It is an ancient form, and it is without a clear base. It seems suspended on the far side of a vast and swallowing chasm.

You must get there.

Suddenly you are there.

The fiefdom commands your presence; the chasm quietly bids you to cross. Before attempting to comply, you look back. You are led to believe your journey has not been long, nothing stretches into infinity, and there is no such thing as an abyss. This you learn from the far-off voices of the pebbles, pebbles that have remained in place but continue to speak in foreign tongues that are becoming more familiar, moment by moment. Listening carefully, you hear them say, wavelike, that they were once all things necessary; that they were once people, places, and obstacles; that they were once fire, water, mountains, plantlife, insects, and animals; that they were once all things earthly. Whether you understand it or not, whether you understand them or not, you are directed to turn back to the kingdom, your destination. You do, and you move on.

The chasm is not at all difficult, but in your crossing, you are, moment by moment, stripped of all things worldly. You are naked of all things you once thought important, and soon you find yourself suspended in front of a door with a face anchored by hinges more ancient than time itself. It offers a higher level of divine peace, and if you could remain there forever and a day, this you would do. But you are forbidden to do so.

You are commanded to enter.

You have entered a world all its own.

The eyes are not free to wander. They fall directly on him. He is almost translucent, yet he wears a dhoti. His appendages can't be seen, he does not look quite as command-ing as the voice had suggested, but he is princely and he rules just the same. And that is why you do not take to heart this world of silence riding on his cold and penetrating eyes — eyes that are multiple and are without pupils and are centered in a cloudlike face, forcefully bringing to mind the Father, the Son, and the Holy Ghost.

But it is not what you see; rather, it is that which is about to be revealed that grips you.

In an instant it comes — your past; your history; your self. And there is more. It is with him. You are sure it is the end; you quickly learn that it is not.

There is a reckoning, and, just as suddenly, you are mesmerized by an oncoming aura of loves, friends, and all who have gone before you. They are to join you; you are to join them. There is beckoning all around you. It rises, then, and just as pronounced — he eases your concern by inviting you to rest in a chair that is nestled between what you imagine is a throne and a containment that has no top, bottom, or sides, yet is mountainous with seeds, pits, and fruits from all over the Earth.

After you are seated, and in a voice more serene and reassuring than any ever heard in all of time, he says, Welcome. It is said that I am death. But it is not so. I am Alpha and Omega; I am the Beginning and the End.

Child of God, I am here to give you birth.

In your travels,
Be wary of the seeker of cause,
And nothing but cause.
In him there is no comfort
In the now;
There will be no joy
On the morrow.

Journeying home from the planet Earth, the child Martian inquired of his elder, Father, on Earth I heard it often, and I heard from the mouths of many. What, I beseech you, sire, is the meaning of the 'N' word?

It is an obscenity, my son. It is a vile and derogatory term ascribed to the black race by a tongue-troubled white race.

Are the blacks not troubled by this, my father?

Aye. And they have been for a long time.

Then why don't they do something about it?

They have tried to for years, my son, but as you have seen, the people of Earth do not possess a oneness of mind.

And is it so with the blacks as well? I ask, because I heard the word mainly from them. I've heard it spoken in their greetings, in their anger, and in their times of joy. I heard it even in their word-music, father.

As have I, my son. It is wrong. It fills me with disgust. And why they choose to use such a term, and do it in the manner that they do, is a mystery that escapes the bounds of reason.

Do the blacks have a troubling name for the whites, my father?

They have several, but they are without impact. They have not stood, nor will they stand, the test of time.

Is that important, sire?

Only because of the insipid and satanic insecurities of man.

But, my father, must not one apply logic in name-calling?

Nay, my son; rather, it is the abandonment of logic. I implore you to think. You have just seen Earth's greatest nation. Would your tongue speak of it as a place of logic?

Nay, my father, nay. Even their wars are without logic.

And thus it shall always be, my son. Even should we part the stars and return to Earth in a thousand years, it will be so. The greatest nation will be gone, as will all existing nations, but I am afraid there will always be an absence of logic on Earth.

The greatest nation, gone? Truly, father?

'Tis more than likely, my son. With so much intolerance, the lessening of values, the worshipping of so many false gods and images; so many killings, the lack of brotherhood amongst men, and the threat of weapons of mass destruction, it is hard to see how mankind or his nations can possibly survive.

And will that be the end of humans?

Again, 'tis more than likely. But his kind is sure to rise again. My only hope is that he can save himself by not acting as his predecessor.

But, sire, Earth did show some promise.

What Earth showed you, my son, was a promise unfulfilled.

Then, sire, I am troubled all the more.

Speak.

You say that name-calling shall forever be?

Aye. And name-calling leads to other things. 'Tis a lack of brotherhood, even in the greatest nation, my son."

And, sire, the more demeaning the name, the more secure the caller?

'Tis far wiser to say the more secure the name, the more *insecure* the caller.

Then, my father, it seems to me that the blacks have the advantage.

You are growing to be ever the wise one, my son. But, even so, if what you have in mind should ever come to pass, only then will that word and all such words suffer in the hands of vileness, and in the soonness thereafter shall name-calling pass away. 'Tis a fine way to save a people. It might be an even a better way to save a planet.

To clear the attic of the mind
is to free the cellar of the soul.

She was wealthy. She had a chateau in Monte Carlo, and homes in other places. As she had done in Ibiza, Spain, and the locales that followed, she was packing, this time heading for Marrakesh. It was as if she were running from time itself. In the midst of packing, she looked in the mirror again. She was bitter. As before, she ran her slender fingers along the curvature of her face, and accused time of being the worst kind of thief. She cursed God.

The eyes became furtive, the looks done in paralyzing snatches, as though the mirror had become more cruel and resolute, once again sorely reflecting that she had lost her beauty, and that her physical endowments were things of the past. She was in the deepest throes of torment. Finally she broke down. Why?! She sobbed over and over again, Why?!!

God's Emissary spoke. I am Time, said he. Dry your eyes. Hear me well. And after I have spoken, rest. He waited until her tears had slowed, then said, Dear one, you are as he who has lost virility; youth who has lost innocence. You are as mornings that have lost dawn; days that have lost sunlight. You are as the years that have lost seasons, and centuries that have become known as the ages. All have moved, as must you. All will change again, as will you. Change is but natural order. Just as your lost beauty would not have set well in your face as an infant, neither would the baby's voice ring true from the throat of the adult. All things change; all things move to the rhythms of natural order. It is progression; it is Time's way. I, as Time, am not here to satisfy vanity nor the moment. I am here to fulfill forever and ever.

Close to relief, she asked, In doing what you have to do, must you bring such torment?

Torment, my child, is not in what I have to do, he answered. Rather it is in that which one refuses to accept. It is only through acceptance that one is able to see that no matter what fills the moment, the best is yet to come.

Together they asked, Why is it that the sons and daughters of the ones who are in the high calling of others can often be more wrong than those who are not — say, like the vicars' son or the physician's daughter? Many are the times when they have been led astray. Often have they forsaken the teachings of the exemplar and followed the path of the wrongdoer. Many have done so with abandon and glee, as if blinded by another light, or have trod as if under the spell of the wayward Pied Piper.

Many are they who have become reproachful and spiteful, and live without morals, virtue, or value; some have gone even beneath the depths of depravity and decadence. This they have done, and it bothers them not that they have brought grief and woe to all who cared, shame on the family name. They do not care to hear of, or even be mindful of, the heartbreak and sorrow of all who were close and dear.

He answered, saying, It is because the vicar

and the physician, even the cobbler and the sheepherder and all their kind, have done as decreed: serve in the service of others, knowing that while it is well to raise children, all who walk the Earth must be served, and the day will come when children will be free to do as children will. Some will leave, and despite the strong stamp or fine moldings of home, they will be lost. They will take upon themselves to do so, and neither the piety of the vicar, the wisdom of the physician, the guidance of the sheepherder, nor the deft hands of the cobbler can alter their course. Though infused with pain, the exemplar can only remain in place, ever hopeful for the lost, yet taking measured comfort in the God-granted knowledge that it is as noble to serve the many as it is to raise the few.

Why, asked the doubter,
do you believe in God?
It would be far better,
said the believer,
if you were to ask God
why he believes in me,
and, more important — you.

32

One often forgets the past. It is not completely lost, but enshrouded in a host of yesterdays. It sometimes has a way of becoming as discomforting as the present is lucid.

Often there is pity.

She lived across the river in Brooklyn. She was not young then, and even though she felt spirited when the gang came around, even then she tried to frolic and brush away the years with dance and conversation and sought vainly to please him, her newfound lover of younger years. He was my friend. He was a jolly, rotund, moon-faced twenty-six, and she loved him mightily. He did not love her as much. She suspected it but it did not diminish her love for him. She gave her love in every way she knew how. She would move the heavens to make him happy. She often tried. There were girlfriends for his boyfriends; parties; outings, the works. She did everything short of meeting his parents for the second time. As he, they lived across the river in New Jersey. But they did not like her. She was too worldly, too far gone. She was much too old. And she was a New Yorker. He was a Jerseyite, a small-time Jerseyite. But despite all, at her urging, he took up residence with her, and for years they lived as man and wife; she tasting bliss, he being not quite so disposed.

He remained on the job, but the old home town didn't see much of him, and none of her. To her it was a blessing. The wide, active streets of Brooklyn were a haven, and her heart would find heightened sensations every time she would peer out the window and see the old Chevy with the Jersey plates pulling in front of their first-floor apartment, there at 212 McDowell Street. She would soothe him after a long day's toil; you could see the thankfulness in her eyes, the gratitude in her embrace.

For the most part, the years of cohabitation were not truly sweet ones. He was restless, and crossing the river and coming home to her after the long day's toil became more bothersome than ever. It grew to the point where even her arms became an annoyance. They were not there to embrace. They were there to imprison.

And so his hours grew later; she remained in the window, her eyes hungrily scanning the streets. Her waiting grew longer.

By late evening he would arrive, and the accusations would be justifiably harsh. He gave them credence because sometimes he would be accompanied by the odoriferous alarm of cheap perfume.

As the nights rolled on, the accusations became more stinging, the arguments more violent. She would accuse him with the ancient charge of unfaithfulness, and he, in no uncertain terms, would decry her age. They shouted the most obscene invectives and it was not uncommon to find them fighting long after the midnight hour, and on until dawn. By morning's rise, though, she would be up and in his service, fawning over him, loving the very air he breathed.

I do not know the day, people, but it happened. The old Chevy did not pull in front of the first apartment there at 212 McDowell Street. It did not pull onto any of the streets of Brooklyn. The car did not even return across the river.

As cars have been known to do under the direction of a restless master, it pulled in front of another place. And although the cars have changed through the years, the driver hasn't.

He has been pulling in front of new places ever since.

I spoke to the old one today, after all these years. She is still in the window in Brooklyn; her eyes are still hungrily scanning the streets.

She is still waiting.

She will wait forever.

— Sometimes it is not easy to recall the past. Sometimes it is filled with pity.

When Talmadge was all of eight, he thought he was Superman. In school he used to sit at his desk and daydream about sailing gracefully out the window to rescue his Lois and cradle her up and down Second Street, so that all the boys in school and all the boys in the neighborhood would say, Superman Talmadge done done it again.

But the boys would never say, Superman Talmadge done done it again, because Superman Talmadge had never sailed out the window, and his Lois, a chubby dumpling of eight and a half, was never in need of rescue.

But, people, you cannot stop the dreamer.

One day after school, little Talmadge swaddled his neck with his daddy's only sheet, and paraded up and down the streets.

You ain't no Superman, the boys chorused.

I is.

You ain't.

I is so!

You ain't not!

I is so, too!!

You ain't not, either!! Y'can't lift no train.

I ain't the kinda Superman that can lift no train. I'm the kinda Superman that can fly.

We ain't never seen you fly nowheres.

That's 'cause y'all ain't been lookin'.

We lookin' now, *Superman* Talmadge, they said, again mocking the word Superman.

But it was a challenge, and Superman Talmadge could ill afford to let it pass.

And he didn't.

Like a little Pied Piper, he led the string of little ones from Berry Street, to Beach Street, across the tracks, around Bootsie Boyd's and B. J.'s house, down Mr. Marshall's and Coleman's alley, across Mr. Bucknight's yard, and finally home. He halted the procession in his back yard, aimed a finger to the attic window, and said, Keep your eyes on that there window right up there, Y'unnerstan'?

We unnerstan'.

He left them and went inside. Minutes later Superman Talmadge appeared in the attic window. Two of the little boys cheered, the rest did not. But it did not affect the man of the hour. He stood there proudly, his cape blowing in the wind. Finally, one of the little boys glumly looked up, and said: Anybody can stan' in a attic window with a sheet on.

I ain't stannin' in a attic window with a sheet on, countered Superman Talmadge. I'm stannin' in my super-secret hidin' place with my super-secret cape on.

Don't look like it to me, said one of the boys who had cheered.

Yeah, said another. So far, you ain't doin' nothin' but stannin' in a attic window with a sheet on. Anybody can do that!

Yeah. C'mon, fly — if you gonna fly.

How far y'gonna fly, Supe? chirped one of the boys.

You're gonna find out, when I fly.

Give us a idea, piped the main disbeliever.

I'm gonna fly... I tell you guys, I'm gonna fly from here to the sky.

Well, hurrup, so I can run home an' tell my momma to watch.

I ain't flyin' to suit your momma.

So far, you ain't flyin' to suit nobody, chimed another. You ain't doin' nothin' but stannin' up there. C'mon, fly — IF you really gonna fly.

Yeah, Supe. Fly, if you gonna fly. Don't keep us down here waitin'.

And they all joined in: C'mon, Superman Talmadge, fly! Fly, Talmadge, fly... fly! Be a *real* Superman! ....Fliiiee...!! Fliiieeee...!!

On they went. They would not stop. Fliie...Flieee...Fliiee...Superman Talmadge! Fliiieee....!! Fliiieee....!!!.

To halt the barrage, Talmadge shot his arms out from his sides. Only then did the boys fall silent. And for a moment, so did the man of the hour. Suddenly, his whole body went rigid.

Then, for all the world to hear, he yelled:

S-S-SHAAA-ZAMMM!!

And it was all over.

...When the ambulance growled to a stop, the attendant hopped out and elbowed his way through the circle of little onlookers and knelt beside the fallen one. He knew better — he knew much better, but with care he asked, Are you all right, sonny?

Superman Talmadge slowly opened his eyes and looked up at the attendant. His face glistening with beads of sweat, his eyes filled with hope, he parted his lips with effort. His voice was almost beneath a whisper. Tell me something, mister... D-d-did I... d-d-did I fly?

The attendant shook his head sadly, No, son, You didn't fly. Little boys aren't meant to fly. Little boys are meant to do many things. But flying is not one of them.

But he did fly, mister, corrected one of the little boys, anxiously looking around for support while tugging on the kneeling man's arm. Guys, didn't we see Supe fly?

Yeah, we saw 'im, they said, almost in unison, and almost to each other. We saw 'im fly. Superman Talmadge *flew*. All'a us guys saw 'im fly. Didn't we see 'im fly, guys?

Yeah! they chorused even louder, vigorously nodding their heads to each other. Talmadge flew! He really *really* flew! We all saw 'im fly! Superman Talmadge flew! He really *really flew!!*

As they continued in exultation, hopping around and cheering for their hero, the little boy known as Superman Talmadge smiled and closed his eyes for the very last time. He knew — even as you and I should know —

You cannot stop the dreamer.

It has caught up with the times. Still, even before landing it looked marshy. It is Monday; it is 5:27 PM in New Orleans. How are you?

It has changed in many ways, but you have a tendency to consult your mental diary and go all the way back to that first-time visit. In it you wrote: It is an ancient place, this city that light-fingered the Mardi Gras from the good people of Mobile, Alabama in the 1800s, yesterday will not easily surrender to tomorrow. It is not odd to find that lifeless grass has rooted itself where sidewalks are supposed to be. It is not odd to find streets with sagging backs and avenues with declining postures. They say that this is the home of the blues, that it is the cradle of true Americana; that music cannot reign in the world of authenticity unless flavored with a taste of New Orleans; that even the winds lay siege to melody and, on a good day, hum of the gaiety of jazz and Dixieland. They say, walk

down any street and the little kinky-haired boy
with the pep in his step and rhythm in his soul
will be tomorrow's Louis Armstrong; the little
spindly-legged girl with the big voice will be your
next Bessie Smith. Travel the other streets,
they say, and surely you will find your Red
Navarros, your Pete Fountains; then, circling
back, find your W. C. Handys; your Twelfth
Street Rags; your musical Americana.

It is unkind to shatter an illusion, but in the
name of accuracy it must be done.

Here, the winds hum of nothing. There is
no dancing in the street; there are no mournful
horns, no hot licks of Dixieland, no kinky-haired
boy tooting his horn, no sounds from the musi-
cally-inclined. Even in expanding your search,
you will not find your W. C. Handys, your
Bessie Smiths, your Louis Armstrongs, your
Twelfth Street Rags; you will not find musical
Americana. And Bourbon Street? Famed
and revered Bourbon Street is but another
tired and littered street in a city of antiquity

and squalor, even though there is newness here.

The city moves about as all others. There are few peculiarities.

There are the Creoles; the gumbo; the Mardi Gras. There is, too, evidence of the South — the old woman sitting on the porch with the dense, cotton stockings rolled just below the knees; the aimlessly strolling man with the soiled cocked cap contrasting with faded overalls; the shuffling of the old; the decrying of an integrated tomorrow.

It is a complex thing, you noted in your mental diary back then. You said New Orleans will not easily surrender to tomorrow. But you also noted: things will change. And on this long-delayed visit, you are quick to note things have changed. It is all to the good.

New Orleans reminds you of a great and determined country. Like Mobile, Alabama, now with the big battleship USS Alabama poised in a vast and beautiful bay as though daring anyone to steal anything from her again, New Orleans reminds you of America.

The Dakotas, the Carolinas, New York, New Jersey, Virginia, West Virginia. Despite the double-jointed names, any parent, police, or authority will tell you, in some ways they are not so very much different from any other.

From the kind climes of Bangor, Maine: Good morning.

When Bobby was just a little tot,
and spat in the neighbor's eyes,
Said his mother to the authorities:
Why, he's just a little child.
When Bobby grew and went to school,
and gave the teacher a whack,
Said his mother to the authorities:
There's no need to overreact.
When Bobby held little Susie's
head down in the pool,
Said his mother to the authorities:
He was just trying to keep her cool.
When Bobby went a-shopping

and stole a bag of toys,
Said his mother to the authorities:
You know, boys will be boys.
And when Bobby grew a little older,
and tried to steal a car,
Said his mother to the authorities:
You know how youngsters are.
Then when Bobby rolled his first joint,
and was trying to find cloud nine,
Said his mother to the authorities:
He was just seeking peace of mind.
Ah, but when Bobby turned to rob-
bery, and was effecting his getaway,
Said the authorities to his mother:
— *Guess who got his today.*

The subway moves beneath the surface like an unrelenting monster. On board, the moods are many. And so are the faces. They come in all shapes, they represent all things.

It is high-noon in New York City. Hi, there.

One looks around haltingly and the eyes' first stop are on a rabbi. Unable to penetrate his beard, the eyes come to rest on the graying man of color with an obvious mental defect. He is not very old, but he is a slender alcoholic, with lips attesting to years of caressing countless bottles. His dark skin and decaying teeth make his mouth look even larger. His bulging, maroon eyes and pulsating neck veins compete with each other as he strains to out-sing the clanking of the subway.

He stops for a moment to allow his eyes to reflectively travel the interior of this mass of metal. There is a Latin face, a Middle Eastern face, a European face, the faces of the aged, the young, the hopeless — and a lone woman of hope. Singing again, the alcoholic stands briefly, rocks with the train, then stops singing to make an announcement. He is loud. Very loud. I'm a longtime vet. I was in 'Nam, fightin' for all'a you people. An' I got medals up the ying-yang to prove it. But I'm really a singer. A tenori. I'm better'n Caruso, Ziliani, Melchior, D'Alessio, Lanza, Pavarotti — all of 'em put together. I can out-sing all of 'em. 'Specially that Pavarotti. All'a y'all hear how good I am. An' if you wanna know the truth, I should be singin' at the Met! Yeah! I should be in the Metropolitan Opera, doin' my thing. I shudda been on Broadway, doin' my thing! Y'all here me?!

No one pays him any attention. He doesn't care. He sits down, singing louder than before.

Slightly up front and across from him, there is pretended sophistication on the face of a woman with a portfolio. A stately brunette with liquid green eyes, she is the one with hope.

In her portfolio are her photographs and a

very thin résumé. Feeling the eyes of the alcoholic singer upon her, she shifts uneasily in her
seat. She notices his fatigues, the faded Army
patch on his jacket, the well-worn boots. She
would be the first to admit that she under-
stands him, and his manner of his dress. She
has considerably more than a certain amount
of empathy for him. It is not because of color.

Momentarily dismissing him for the job at
hand, she crosses her legs with an acquired dain-
tiness and sends her fingers wandering across
her lap and clutches her portfolio tighter. Even
though her résumé is thin, she is proud of her
8x10s — pictures that should get her through
the front door and into a world she has been
dreaming about for a lifetime; to be like Sarah
Bernhardt or Helen Hayes, or the more
recent Johanna Morrison whom she saw as the
powerful Regan in Shakespere's King Lear.

After a moment, she frees a hand and pats
at her stiff, coiffured hair. She would like the
world to know she is a star in the making; that

she has what it takes. Although it has been a long time coming — over twenty-some years — she is en route to her first audition; she is Broadway bound. It will be a trip unfulfilled.

As the alcoholic vet could have told her, it is hard to get anyone to believe that you have the makings of a star when you've spent almost a lifetime in the military, as he had.

And as had she.

The vet could have told her, too, that it wasn't his time in "'Nam" or the over twenty years in service to the nation that drove him to drink. It was rejection. Being rejected by the Met, or Broadway — or by any show-business venue is apt to drive any hopeful to drink.

Still, if he would have stopped singing long enough, he would have wished her well.

Talented people do that to each other.

— There is an agonizing screech of metal against metal, and the train comes to a halt. The doors methodically open, and there is a changing of the guard in subterranean New York.

Greetings. It is topical and remote — and still unable to vote for the President of the United States. It is vitally strategic to the nation's present interests in the Pacific, three times the size of D.C., has a population of 157,556, of which most are Chamorroans and Filipinos, was ceded to the U.S. by Spain in 1898, captured by the Japanese in 1941, and was retaken by U.S. forces three years later.

It is the Territory of Guam.

He had written the speech at the Repple Depot in Seattle, Washington, but it is here where the newly-appointed Commanding General rehearsed it for eventual delivery to the conquered.

In 1945 he got his chance.

His delivery to the defeated people was strong and flawless. At the height of it he said: We want nothing more than to acquaint you with the virtues of democracy. We want nothing more than to decentralize your government, eliminate imperialism, and show you the American way of life. The war is over. We are the victors, but you are the beneficiaries. We will show you brotherhood and the ability of a peace-loving people to get along with each other despite our sociological differences, or any other differences we may or may not have.

Democracy is brotherhood; justness; equality. It is the respect we have for each other. Imperialism has misled you. Democracy is the American way; it is the only way. This is our creed; this is our true calling.

And on he went.

When the speech was over, an aide gently inquired, Sir, does that mean Negro troops will now serve with whites?

What, demanded the general, ever gave you that ridiculous idea?

The great state of Ohio. East of the Great Lakes, fought hard for the North; home of Ulysses S. Grant and William Sherman. Not too toursy; clings to tradition. Excuse me for whispering, but his campaign is not going well. He is behind in the polls and it's close to election day and they are readying the cameras for the last go-round. He needs a hook in a hurry; a stronger theme; a better sound bite. He needs something to energize the people.

Ahem. Greetings again. It is two days before the election and it appears he's found what he's been looking for, and he's not giving the speech. He's living it. Sleeves rolled up, pounding on the podium, sweating profusely, he's on a roll: And I say again, people; it is shameful the way we are treating our black brothers and sisters. The Constitution guarantees these people certain inalienable rights, yet we have failed them. When we can spend billions on a tragic war and neglect those residing in the pockets of poverty, then it's high-time for us to take a closer look at ourselves. Where, I ask you, is our concern for brotherhood? Where is our concern for a people denied? Where is our concern for a people who are unable to sup on the fruits of this great nation? I don't know about you, but I am severely troubled by this, and I have no intention of resting until something is done to help the oppressed.

When I assume office, I will not rest until these people denied have infiltrated every facet of society, I will not rest until we have disbanded every ghetto, leveled every playing field, elevated every neighborhood. I will not rest until the blacks — and all the unfortunates in this country are able to rise up and take their rightful place in the mainstream of America.

And when he went home his wife greeted him with a bright and cheery: Oh, honey! Guess who moved in next door?

— It is sad, indeed, to see a politician cry.

Good morning. It is known for its chowder and its rich food from deep waters. But it should be appreciated for much more. You think about its history and what it has meant to the nation. You're glad it's here; you're glad to be here. It has problems. It has many problems, but it is a great city, Boston is.

He was a traveler and a former justice of the superior court. A quiet gentleman of bearing, he was fastidious in his dress, a stickler about his food. In one of the more famed restaurants, it appeared that he was having trouble making up his mind. The waiter suggested having tongue for lunch, saying that it was broiled to perfection, and that his European chef used only the finest herbs and spices.

Replied the former justice to the waiter, and in no uncertain terms, My good man, it matters not how you broil it, bake it, roast it or toast it; it mattersd not what spices, herbs or or condiments you may use or disuse. Tongue is still tongue. It is the second filthiest part of a cow, and I presume you have at least a remote idea as to what the first part is. Do you realize that everything a cow eats starts with the tongue? Have you ever seen a live cow's tongue? — or even a dead one, for that matter. A cow's tongue is the longest and nastiest thing you've ever seen. It's constantly dripping with saliva, and there's not a bacteria on the planet that doesn't make a home on it. And do you know where that bacteria goes, and what filthy part of the cow it eventually comes out of? It's disgusting!

Then, what may I order for you, sir?

Ham and eggs, said the former justice, adjusting his bib, then moving his chair closer to the table. Eggs, sunny-side up. Milk on the side.

Aerodynamically, a bee is not supposed to fly. But it does, and it does so most efficiently. Yet, from a certain point of view, the most confounding thing to take to the air is the airplane. Save for the clouds, nothing can match it. Going or coming, it exudes effortless beauty. It is a tribute to man's endless reach.

He was enthusiastic about immigrating to the country where freedom reigned supreme and when the limo driver picked him up at the airport, he had many questions. Then came the question of the American white woman.

The answer was like something Jerry Boyd would have said. The American white woman is the single-most privileged somebody to ever walk the face of the Earth. In the superbowl of life, she was born on the fifty yard line, had the goalposts move up to the twenty, and can score six points on a field goal.

That is football?

Our national obsession, said the driver.

What would you say about the white man?

I'd say forget him. There's a flag on the play.

And the blacks?

Delusional, said the driver. Still on the outside, looking in, wondering why God hasn't called the game on account of darkness.

So the white woman is the thing?

She is not the "thing," kind sir. She's the game. Everything here revolves around her jolly, little bouncing buns.

Oh, my, said the immigrant, his brow knitted with concern. Er, would you be good enough to do a double left at the corner.

Why? said the driver. That'll take us back to the airport.

I certainly hope so, said the immigrant. And the sooner I'm on a plane, the better off we'll all be.

It tries to shy away from the notoriety, but it sometimes bustles with big-city activity. It is shortly before 10:30 PM in Des Moines, Iowa.

Jake's Place is jammed with customers. There is also hammering coming from the rear.

It is more than a tad disconcerting. Excuse me while I go for a pit stop.

ONLY ONE CUSTOMER AT A TIME

It is the sign of the times, and bar-owner Jake is nailing it onto the men's room door with unrestrained vigor.

He has his reasons.

On the other side of the men's room door, the gays had been inserting their rights. Now he is asserting his.

A sublime and munificently gorgeous sun-swept day in a city that has it all. Looking back, or looking forward, if the winds of winter weren't so fierce and angry, this could have very well been America's most populous city. Despite some serious misgivings, still it is a great and vibrant city, Chicago is. And it is ever so typi-cal of the USA. Everyone here claims to own it; no one wants to pay for it.

He had soft eyes and pillowy dimples that were nestled in a cherubic face accented by a head full of magnificent hair. There was no doubt about it, he was a cute little thing, and no one was more aware of it than his mother.

But to the doting mother, the little one was not simply cute; the word was too inadequate, beautiful would not do, and the term "glorious" was only scratching the surface. He was all. He was her sunrise, her sunset, her bright and last-ing star. Sometimes she would do nothing but

sit and stare and while away the hours marvel-
ing at his preciousness, and though, at times,
there would be silence, the love communicated
would be as pronounced and eloquent as any
the world has ever known.

There was a third party. He loved them
both; he loved them dearly.

But the third party would come home at
day's end and suffer the indignity of being ig-
nored. There was no love for him, no words for
him — nothing for a husband and father who
had been reduced to the role of the intruder.

He was severely bothered by the treatment, but it was only out of loving concern for
the two of them that he cautioned her against
over-devotion to the little one.

She accepted him and his words as a form
of mental cruelty and took her case to court.

The judge agreed with her; the divorce was
granted. Now, by law, the intruder went his
separate way; there was nothing to obstruct a
mother's love for the young and tender.

And nothing did.

Who do you love most in the whole wide world? went the daily ritual.

He would smile and brush his little nose up against hers, and say, You, Mommie. And I want to be just like you when I grow up.

I saw him the other day. His wish had been granted.

— Nylon stockings and all.

Big Stone Gap, Virginia. Not too stimulating; not exactly the place to catch a breather before moving on, but it's the place to be if you want to see the unhip but long-running outdoor drama, Trail of the Lonsome Pine.

The streets are quiet and cozy, and the night settles easily.

Mr. Clark would not have done well here.

One is not too sure about Miss Pearl.

Mr. Clark was poor, but Miss Pearl was poorer. He owned the local grocery store; she was a loyal customer. Sometimes she he would enter the store, see a slice of meat that she wanted, squint at her crumpled dollars and sparse pennies, and in a kind and grandmotherly voice ask, Mr. Clark, could you trim the fat off the meat before you weigh it?

In an equally kind and soft voice, he would say, I'd like to, Miss Pearl, but I don't peel the potatoes before I weigh them.

It was always something to that effect, and they both had grown used to it. For years there had been a contest between them. But the odds were in his favor. The store's scale was tilted and was not accurately balanced, and a pound was not really a pound. A pound on his scale was half a pound anywhere else, and, too, Mr. Clark was touched with the habit of placing a slab of meat or a bag of groceries on the tilted old scale and the pressure of his thumbs would be generously included in the price. It was a way of life; it was no surprise.

It was no surprise, either, that when the new supermarket opened on Main Street most of the customers were more than quick to desert the old store. But the likes of Miss Pearl could not afford the luxury of getting on a bus and going all the way to Main Street. And so she remained. Mr. Clark thanked her for her loyalty, but his thanks did not affect the pressure of his thumbs, and to compensate for the lack of customers, he pressured the scale even more.

But pressuring the scale was not enough. And so one day Mr. Clark regretfully informed the old lady that he was closing his doors for the last time. It was a sad day. He wanted to tell her that Main Street was not going to like her shopping habits, but the words would have sounded harsh, and so he said nothing. She wanted to tell him that she was afraid of the giant store, and that she was not going to like it because there were sure to be more scales and more thumbs. But the words would have sounded harsh, and so she said nothing.

And so it was on to Main Street.

Unhappily, they both were correct in their thinking. She was right because there were indeed more scales and many more thumbs, and she was afraid. The old grocer was right because they did not like her shopping habits.

— No matter how soft the voice or grandmotherly the ways, supermarkets just don't take kindly to shoplifting old ladies.

Montreal, Canada. Crisp air. Clean, alluring, and nicely cosmopolitan.

But not everyone has been so touched.
He is ragged and shoeless. He is unsteady on his feet. He slurs his words and ambles the streets, spilling pearls of wisdom to anyone who cares to listen. I do, however, like his rhythm.

Here comes the darkness men
done cuss'd,
Methinks things could be a whole
lot wuss'd.
S'posin' the darkness comes, an' t'was here
to stay —
An' we'd never get the chance to see
the day.
Stumblin' an' grumblin' all thru
the nights —
We can't make it without
d'lights.

Moving on to Vancouver, where he would wake up and meet the boys around the barrell for a morning sip from a bagged bottle of wine. This morning he refused to budge.

Woke up early dis mornin'
An' I heard d'news,
They's shootin' at the moon,
    They gonna blow out d'fuse.
Don't know'd nothin' 'bout no
    Outer space
But what they doin'
    Can't be safe.
Fools lookin's for somethin'
    to attack —
S'posin' they hit the moon
    An' the moon hit back?
Gonna go back to bed,
    Gonna bury my head.
Damn if I wanna
    Wake up dead.

The Motor City. A worthy, but minor disappointment. The economy, however, is on the rebound. And so is Michigan optimism.

In this, the birthplace of the auto, it is a cheerfully bright and sunny day at the bus stop.

...Well, I'll be! Why, if you ain't a sight for sore eyes!

Ha, ha, ha, same as you. An' look at you! Lookin' good! How you been, boy?

Can't kick. Bone's a lil' sore. Arthritis talkin' to me a li'l bit. Other than that, everythin's fine. You lookin' well.

Been feelin' well. Ain't had too much trouble since I saw you last. Come to think of it, it's been quite a spell since we bumped into each other.

Say, y'know, you're right. It has been a spell. When was the last time I saw you?

Lemme see, now...was it back in —?

No. Wait, I got it. I saw you back in —

Seems to me I saw you 'fo then. I saw —

No. T'won't then. Oh, I know when it was when we saw one 'nother.

No, I see'd you since then.

You see'd me since — ? Say, that's right!

Yeah. R'member we saw each other down by the old — ?

Come to think of it, you're right. S'been so long, I almost forgot. Well, you certainly ain't changed none. I see you lookin' as fit as a fiddle.

An' you ain't lookin' too bad y'self. Y'brother still livin'?

He's still aroun'. Saw him last summer. Howz your family doin'?

Lost a few. But some of 'em's still kickin'. I see 'em every now an' then. — Ooops, I see my bus is comin', gotta shove off.

Well, sure was good seein' you again.

An' good seein' you, too. Take care of yourself.

— They waved goodbye, and the two blind men departed.

As they said from the start, they were a sight for sore eyes.

It was 2:45 AM when the plane touched down. Not much movement since then. Everything is fine, except the wee hours has escorted one of those hard, lightning-laced summer storms to Houston. The cabs are running slow. There is nothing to do except sit, wait, and look at the sleep-starved people.

The queen just left.

Indeed, she was queenly. Complete with glittering slippers and a matching purse, she was dressed as if heading for the ball. She stood at the terminal door, peering through the thick glass as though awaiting her coach. It did not disturb her, that thick, Texas-accented voice that resonated all the qualities of a twice-denied hog-caller as it droned over the speakers, announcing the arriving and departing flights with dead-of-night boredom. She dismissed it and everything around her in an air of isolated sophistication.

Her mind, no doubt, was locked on her coach.

Through the glass she could see the reflection of an army of eyes in motion after being positioned in an area conducive to watching beauty from the rear.

Many who passed stopped to offer her a ride, but she wouldn't budge. The icy regality held at the door, and one was left with the feeling that anything less than the arrival of a gilded chariot to pick her up would be an assault on royalty.

And then it happened. Her mode of travel arrived. It waited dutifully.

With a porter trailing with her luggage, she waltzed to the curb and was smothered with tight hugs and kisses by her apparent lover. And together the two women rode off into the night.

— Truly, it was like Love's Old Sweet Song, except the coach was a truck.

It would be nice, said the dog to the hog, resting easy in the old barnyard, if we could get humans to stop calling each other dogs and pigs.

Overhearing it was the snake. Said he to the coon, casting an eye on the donkey:

...And they think they've got a problem.

San Diego. Arguably it provides a worthwhile function, this world-renowned zoo does. But one would like to know just how deeply the animal longs for the freedom of the plains. Also, one wouldn't mind asking the monkeys about a certain party their buds were supposed to have hosted on the plains of the Serengheti.

The story goes, when they used to be bold,
    the monkeys up'd and gave a feast.
They sent out cards with their kind regards,
    to every kind of bird and beast.
On a leg that was lame, still the buzzard came,
    and said, am I first upon the scene?
No, said the snake, you're just a li'l bit late,
    I'm here, and in my best blue jeans.
And for your edification (means your information) arriving next was Ms. Porcupine.
Then came the stork, with knife and fork,
    and the piggies won't far behind.
Came the orangutan and another strange

thing, followed by a zebra and a deer;
Then a hippo and a rhino, blowing kisses to a
llama, talkin' trash in an elephant's ear.
The ol' grizzly bear, with a part in his hair,
said, what a thing we got goin' here!
I see a kangaroo, a gorilla, too;
I see's they comin' from far and near.
Then up crawled a crab, who gave her eyes a dab,
And nodded to the coon(y)
He said: Hello cow, evenin' crow,
An' what's shakin' with the ol' baboon(y).
But going away from the feast, sailing high
were the geese,
and looking up was a sweet-talking lion.
He said, hey, li'l birdy, didn't you get the
monkey's wordy?
The party's on the ground and y'all is flyin'.
Said the geese to the lion: We gonna keep on
flyin', we gonna stay out'a your way,
With your real nasty habits, once you sweet-
talked some rabbits, Lawd, they never lived
another day.

An' like the wise old owl told all us fowl,
   Let the monkeys go and have their feast.
Let 'em party as they please, pretty soon they
gonna see's, that a beast ain't nothin' but a beast.
   The ol' crocodile forced a big, bright smile,
   When the alligator grabbed a plate.
He said, listen, monk, it's time to break bread,
   I gets touchy when my din-din's late.
But up stepped a canis lupus, sayin' I ain't one
to raise the roofus,
   But I'm new king of all the beasts,
   S'nice to have a rumble for the boys in the
jungle, but don't count on havin' no feast.
   I ain't one to boast, but I done ate the host,
now all y'all better scram.
   I got a appetite that still ain't right,
   Hungry yet I am.
But said the lion to the group, still hungering
for some soup,
   Wolf didn't really make a meal of the monks.
If the monkeys lost their nerve, let the alliga-
tors serve, or put some aprons on the tail-

raised skunks.

But said the coon to the lion, Sir, the alligator's cryin', and not a drop is a crocodile tear;

With a nose that long, he can tell if somethin's wrong, so, somethin's really, really wrong 'round here,

'Cause the only ol' beast ain't waitin' on the feast is the wolf with his ol' toothpick;

That ain't the way he was lookin' 'fo the monkeys started cookin', Sir, I'm 'bout to get awfully sick.

Said the buzzard to the hog and a sad-eyed dog, sheddin' tears with the old jackass;

I say you never will be able to get a wolf around a table, 'Cause he never did have no class.

Once we was all in the woods, pickin' bones an' other goods, we heard the voice of a sweet, young thing;

With her red-frocked fanny, she was off to see her granny, An' the itty bitty voice did sing:

A tisket, a tasket, I've got my Granny bas-

ket: An' I'm singin' in the woods.
Lawd, the wolf turned his back, an' said, I kind'a
likes that...

Y'all remember Red Ridin' Hood.
Ooops, ooops, ooops, said the jackal on the
run, don't let me spoil nobody's fun,

but I see's the wolf ain't one to play.
If he attacked Ms. Hood, an' she was singin'
that good, I say it's time to make my getaway.

An' if y'all think he ain't straight 'bout who
he said he ate, take a look behind the pot where
he was.

If you see a trace of any monkey's face,
Then you lookin' in a mirror, that's what.

But what you ought'a do, is take your li'l
cue from the lion that's streakin' ahead.

If he's the king of the jungle, an' the wolf
has got him runnin'

Then there ain't nothin' else to be said.

New Mexico. Harmony saturating lazy air. Golden hues. It's going to be one of those splendid, uplifting, God-on-the-job kind of days in a bland but cozy little town called Truth or Consequences. Good Morning.

On the faraway plains an ant emerged from a dusty burrow, yawned, stretched, and intoned, What a great day for going on a leisurely stroll or small jaunt.

A gnat of dubious mental stability happened to be fluttering within hearing distance responded, A jaunt? After going scuba-diving, I was on my way to inquire about taking piano lessons to sate my love for music. But what a lovely idea you have. Perhaps we can jaunt together. I love traversing the soil with ants.

'Tis a lovely notion, my fine fellow, replied the ant. But you are with wings, I am with feet. There is no way we can jaunt together.

Aaaah, the gnat generously yielded. You

are with many feet. But what if I do as I've done with other ants? What if I don't use my wings and use only my feet? In such a way we can be together.

Beautiful thinking, said the ant. Alight yourself, kind sir, and a'jaunting we shall go.

Off they went, with the impish gnat enthusiastically chatting about taking piano lessons, with his ultimate aim being to master the grand piano. He breezed past various ambitions, then chatted about how he enjoyed being in the company of ants. The only trouble was, they had a tendency to disappear. They were like the notes of music, he said.

The ant listened attentively, and was about to ask how a gnat went about the most peculiar act of learning how to play a piano — particularly a grand piano — when they approached a stretch of highway. His attention diverted, he said, We'd better not attempt a crossing. Let us walk paralleling the road for a spell, then we shall veer off into another direction and continue our jaunt.

But there is much to see on the other side of the road, replied the gnat. I have flown over there many times. As I told the other ants, there are fields of dandelions, strawberry patches, flowers — everything for us to enjoy on such a fine and healthy day. There's cotton over there that even the boll weevils and gophers don't know anything about. You're sure to love it.

Very intriguing indeed, said the ant. But the road is ripe with danger. I see none now, but this is a highway of cars that are as fast as lightning and trucks that are as big as houses. If we aren't crushed by the tires, the winds alone will blow us from here to China. For us to even think about a crossing on foot is most foolhardy.

That's why God gave certain species wings — to fly out of harm's way, responded the gnat.

Good for you, bad for me, said the ant.

Good for the both of us, countered the gnat, exuberantly. As I have done for other ants, I shall use my wings, and from a position in the air I shall act as an observer. If the road is clear, I will give a signal, and you can cross.

But if the cars are as fast as lightning and the trucks are as big as houses, and I am in the middle of the road, your signal will be of no use.

Then I shall position myself higher in the air, which will enable me to see even further up and down the road, thus allowing me more communication time. I shall rise like the notes of music.

Good thinking, said the ant. By the by; what did the other ants say when you helped them cross the road?

That's the one strange thing I find about ants. I lead them to the start of the crossing, then I never hear anything else from them. I'd love to find out why.

It truly is strange, replied the ant. Generally, we are such a grateful lot.

I've always thought so, replied the gnat. But I never hear from them. It really puzzles me.

Well, when I get across, you can be sure you'll hear from me.

The gnat thanked him, and, as he had done for the other ants, he put his wings into motion and lifted himself up. From a nice position high in the air, he started scanning the road. Then he went higher. Suddenly his wings started fluttering with urgency. The ant took it as a signal and started his crossing. But no sooner had he done so than a monster-sized, 18-wheeler truck came thundering his way. It was only through the greatest of all miracles that the ant was able to escape to the other side of the road with his life.

When the gnat zoomed to the prostrate ant's side, he was overjoyed. Congratulations! he exclaimed. What a remarkable achievement! Glorious! How does it feel to be on this side of the road??

Still trembling and gasping, the ant said, Are you crazy?! You almost cost me my life, signaling me like you did!

I wasn't signaling you, the gnat protested. I was signaling the driver, trying to get him to slow down. Like I did for the other ants.

You are a gnat! An insect! A man driving an 18-wheeler truck can't see a gnat!

Ah-hah! exclaimed the gnat. Now I know why I never heard from the other ants.

Because the ants are dead, you bobble-headed nut!! They're dead, dead, dead!! They're dead because a truck driver can hardly see a gnat on the ground, let alone one flying in the air!! And they never *will* be able to *see* a gnat flying in the air!!

Ah, then we shall have the last word, my friend. For I shall make the great sacrifice, postured the gnat. Instead of me learning how to play the piano, for our next jaunt, I shall learn how to *carry* the piano.

It was a time of civil disobedience in the country, and he was a man of peace. Some were
saying, America. Love it or leave it. The mili-
tants were saying, America. Change it or lose
it. But the man of peace was of a different
mindset. He believed in the nation's creed. He
spoke, inspired, and led his marches in the name
of freedom. Then one day he was felled by an
assassins' bullet. The nation was in shock, but
not everyone mourned his passing. His detrac-
tors dug deep, and many unkind things were
unearthed about him, and many young people
were hurt. Rebecca was one of them. She had
deified the man; elevated him to the divine pla-
teau of sainthood. Now she was worried about
his afterlife. Based on what she had heard, her
saint was not even going to pass through to
the Gates of Heaven. In tears, she went to her elder.

Said he to her: If you were God, Rebecca,
and two men stood before you in judgement,
and one man said: Ma'am; in the year 1776, I
was a holder of slaves, but I fostered a cause
and fathered a nation, and today, as I stand

before you, I am pround to say, my work is done. For that nation is the greatest nation on Earth.

And if the other man standing before you said: Ma'am; two hundred years later, in the shadows of this man's monument, in the great city that bares his name, I, too, fostered a cause, and I tried to raise that great nation's conscience. But, today, as I stand before you, I am sad to say, my work is yet undone.

Now, my dear Rebecca, if you were God — and mind you, it is altogether possible womankind serves in ways yet unknown to man — but if you were God, which of these godly servants would you invite to sit beside you?

The pigtailed young Miss thought for a moment, then said, I'd choose both of them, if I could. Dr. King and George Washington. But, sir, they're saying Dr. King did some bad things in his personal life. He was not perfect.

Neither was George, said the elder. None of us are perfect, and neither George nor Martin were supposed be. Try to remember, perfection suggests completeness; and only God is complete.

And speaking of the kiddies,
said the jackal to the owl,
How many little ones did
the donkey give birth to this time?
I don't know, replied the owl,
But you can be sure
they are all asses.

94

San Francisco. Capital of the West.

He was unusual; the salt of the earth. He did not like artificiality. The one he chose had to be as God had intended, as nature had adorned. But in a cosmeticized world such as ours, he knew she would be slow in coming.

And she was.

Time pushed many across his path, but he was not to weaken. They were not for him. His acquaintances eyed him suspiciously and one by one they fell out of touch. Time, too, slipped by him; he grayed, and he was bent a little. It looked as though he would perish without ever having mated. But then one day he saw her. Hers was windswept beauty. She was gracefully raw and uncluttered; a child of nature, the essence of purity.

He had to have her.

It took time, lots of time, but it finally happened. An elegant night was theirs. They strolled the wharf, then, over dinner, violins

played in hushed tones; romance filled the air.
Gently, over the soft candlelight, he whispered,
I am captivated by your unpretentiousness,
hypnotized by your natural beauty. You come
to me more luminous than the stars, and fresher
than a morning sunrise. There is not an artifi-
cial thing about you or your body. And your
hair — ah, that glorious, glorious, heart-stop-
ping hair. It has the sheen of moonlight shim-
mering on delicate waters.

Do you really like it? she asked, breath-
lessly.

I adore it, my love, said he.

I'm glad you do, she cooed. I just bought it.
And I'm thinking about having it dyed.

Missouri, the *Show Me* state. The State Insect is a honey bee, the State Instrument, a fiddle. Better to think about Harry Truman, the 33rd U.S. President, or even Mark Twain.

There is a man-made wonder here. It's called the Gateway Arch. You wonder how they built it. It's like when you were in South Dakota a few days back and saw the magnificent Mt. Rushmore. You keep asking yourself, how did somebody even *think* of it. Howdy.

On the subject of building something.

They wanted to tear the little church down. In its place, they wanted to build an edifice that stretched from block to block to block. They wanted the pastor to speak from a pulpit that would outdo all others, and where the parishioners could sit on cushioned pews and see him from all angles. They wanted a rotunda. There was criticism from more than a few, and, said a deacon, This has all the makings of a building to glorify man, which we should not do. Our cause is to glorify the Creator.

The Creator deserves the best that we can give Him, countered the pastor. If He didn't want us to build a place where I can be heard and seen from all angles, He wouldn't have been so generous. Thanks to my preaching and His blessings, we have funds aplenty to build something new and glorious. The Creator deserves to have His word preached in the best church; the finest that man can provide. If He decided to send His Son back to Earth today, don't you think He would be riding in the best car? He wouldn't be riding on what was prominent when He created Heaven and Earth. Jesus would be riding and spreading the word from the Rolls Royce of his day, and from what, I might generously add, you continue to be by arguing with me.

Said the deacon, The Rolls Royce of Jesus' day was an ass.

— Precisely, said the pastor.

Coeur d'Alene, Idaho. Good Evening.
From the clear, deep blue water's edge to the clean, clean Fair Grounds and beyond — everywhere you look — sweeping vistas; Chamber of Commerce beauty.

It ruined the illusion to hear him ask the question.

Goin' out tonight?
asked the nightlifer.
Can't, replied the Reverend.
Tomorrow's Sunday. Gotta preach.

It ruined the illusion even more, because they were standing in front of a church.

New Hampshire. Picturesque; old America. First state to declare independence, and proud of it. Aloof, outdoorsy, sells whiskey on Sundays, and is happy because of it.

It could use some paint, but it's still quaint and unique. It has an inspirational cross that dominates a deeply slanted roof and aims for the heavens. It has all the New England charm and character one would want.

Hello, there. It is quiet and serene here.

Inside the little wooden building is a different matter. The air is taut; matters are getting down to the crucial point. The kind old ladies with beaded purses and blue-rinsed hair have their eyes riveted on their cards.

B-2!
Silence.
I-24!
Silence.
O-71!

Silence.

N-37!

Silence.

G-50!

How was that again?

G-60!! Sorry.

Thank you.

O-75!

Suddenly someone shouts: B-B-BINGO!!

Someone else shouts, OH, S---!!

— Clearly, playing bingo in a serene little church does not bring out the best in people.

Home of USC Trojans football, one-time home of the L.A. Dodgers, Rams, and Raiders; host of the first and seventh Superbowl games, site of the Olympics in '32 and '84, and the place where 134,254 souls assembled for a Pope's visit a few years back. Its doors swung open in '24, and it is listed on the National Register of Historical Places.

It is the Los Angeles Memorial Coliseum. And it is huge.

Empty now, but you're sitting high up in the bleachers at the northeast end of the stadium. It is exciting. You can still hear the roar of the crowd; you remember the hysteria.

You would like to see another event, but you wish it could be keep it in perspective. You wish you could hear the coach say, It was neither the Second Coming, a cure, nor miracle. It was a game, guys — *a game*. The poor is still with us, and cancer has yet to be cured.

Baltimore, Maryland. Not a high-flyer, but a proud city of spunk and determination. For contrast, it has a tremendous aquarium, and a solid deep-water port. It also has a noble history. I favor its House of Delegates; I favor the ever-hopeful Morgan State University.

The fight is not over; indeed, the fight will never be over, and many cities would like to make the claim, but in the all-important area of Civil Right, no American city has done more to foster equality. We owe a debt to Baltimore.

Washington gave his farewell address here.

It is also the birthplace of the Star Spangled Banner.

En masse they came; en masse they spoke:

Your company is hypocritical; not a single one of your employees is black.

The company hired one.

They came back. Your company is guilty of tokenism; only one of your employees is black.

The company hired two more.

They came back. Your company is only window-dressing, only three of your employees are black.

The company hired three more.

They came back. Your company ain't even close to fillin' the quota; only six of your employees are black.

The company hired six more.

They came back. Your company is backslidin' on progress; only twelve of your employees are black.

The company hired twelve more.

They came back. Your company ain't smellin' the roses; only twenty-four of your employees are black.

The company hired twenty-four more.

They came back. Your company is layin' low on us; only forty-eight of your employees are black.

The company hired forty-eight more.

They came back.

—But the company was gone.

Cape Cod, Cape Hatteras, Cape
Good Hope — name the locale; from here to
south-central Ghana on the gulf of Guinea to
the southern-most province of the Republic
of South Africa to the Province York Penin-
sula or all the way over to Portugal's Verde Is-
lands and on to Nova Scotia's Cape Breton
Island; from deep escarpments to jutting prom-
ontories, from swooping inclines to gentle
slides, they are God's ceaseless wonders.
You've seen them. They are the capes; the
noble blending of Earth's soul and spirit.

Is God dead? asked one.
I should hope so, said the other.
I would surely hate to think
his services are restricted to the living.

It was in the racially turbulent 60s. He was a New York executive. His company was sending him to the backwoods of Georgia on a research trip. As a black man, he was greatly concerned. Georgia was the Peach State, but in his mind and in the minds of many at the time, it was the home of Crackers. The Peach State may not have been the heart of Dixie, but few would have denied that it wasn't the soul.

The flight to the old state was uneventful, but his first encounter wasn't.

Before even boarding the airline shuttle with baggage and briefcase, he had eyed the driver suspiciously. He didn't like him. All the signs were there. Thin lips, narrow chin, slouched and ruddy; the stare of a bigot. The New Yorker had seen his kind on TV, unleashing dogs and aiming water hoses on his people, and spitting vitriol on the children as they tried to integrate a retarded school system.

Where to? drawled the ruddy-faced one.

The Rharl Hotel, said the New Yorker.

The thin, ruddy-faced driver shook his head, Naw. You don't wanna be on this bus.

Well, let me put it to you this way, said the New Yorker. I'm not getting off the bus. So you might as well move the bus, or make your move personally. Move it or lose it. You people down here don't scare me one bit.

The thin one sat lazily in the humidity, added moisture to an already stained cigarette that was hanging from his lips, and waited.

When the last of the airport passengers had climbed aboard, the man threw the bus into gear and nursed it away from the terminal. The New Yorker was still smoldering. Crackers all, he muttered to himself, making it the fifth time he had done so.

It was a long, stop-and-go, dreary ride in a stark night, and they had gotten so far out that they no longer passed lampposts. The New Yorker was certain something was amiss.

It was about an hour later now, and everyone else had long since departed the forty-
three-passenger vehicle. The two of them were
riding in stony silence.

Braced for trouble, the New Yorker had
already slipped a hand into his briefcase and
was fingering his cold snub-nosed .38.

Finally the bus pulled in front of a dimly lit
hotel that was set deep off the road. Like the
road, it was in deplorable shape, and the visitor
from New York couldn't mask his displeasure.

Through the rearview mirror, the thin one
saw his passenger's disappointment. He cut
the interior lights off, opened the door, but
said nothing. The two of them sat for a long
while, then the driver decided to darken his lips
with another roll of stained tobacco.

With heat coming in from the opened door,
and certain that it was a was a setup, the New
Yorker wiped a bead of sweat from his fore-
head and tightened the grip on his pistol.

He was ready.

To break the tension, the driver exhaled a curl of smoke. Friend, he said. I didn't think you wanted the Rharl. As you can see, it ain't one of our finest, and it's just too doggone far out for businessmen. Especially a good-appearin' businessman like yourself.

Head lowered in total embarrassment, the black one sat in a deflated silence. He thought of what he had come close to doing. And he thought of his wife and son back home. Seized by a cold shudder, he said to himself, Misconception. It sure can be a costly thing.

He sat for a while longer, then wondered if the driver had anyone at home whom he cared about. Then, with spirit, he apologized for his conduct and what he had been thinking earlier.

The driver graciously accepted the apology. And the two of them rode back into the heart of town, chatting as only good men can.

— Georgia in the '60s. Home of Crackers. And peaches.

Educated abroad, he was a dyed-in-the-wool elitist; a resident of the nose-bending climes of snooty Beverly Hills, California.

Lower levels did not interest him, he would not see what others saw, and neither would his young son.

Son, counseled he to the little one, Always hold your head up higher than all others, thus your aspirations shall never be mired in the dirt of the Earth.

The son tried holding his head high for a while, but it was soon forgotten.

Son, the father, said again, Hold your head up higher than all around you, thus you shall never see the wrongs of man.

The son tried it for a while, but it was soon forgotten.

Son, the father said again, and far more sternly, Hold your head up high, thus you shall always be above the commoner.

The son tried holding his head high, but it was soon forgotten.

Son, the father demanded, Hold your head up high and you will see things yet untouched.

The son tried it for a while more, but it was soon forgotten.

Son, the father said again, Hold your head up so that you can see and be part of majesty and beauty.

The son tried it for a while longer, but the effort was soon forgotten.

Son, the father said lastly, Keep your head up high and above all others or I shall brace your neck so that you can see nothing but the spaciousness of the sky.

The son tried his best to keep his father's will, but his little neck tired and soon fell back into normalcy.

The father did as he said he would do. He braced his son's neck.

For release, and to soothe the father's ire,

the boy solemnly promised to keep his head high and his eyes planted upward.

He did so, even in the path of a truck.

— Strange, thought the undertaker as he prepared the body for burial. I wonder why the old one wants the little one's head lowered.

Ethereal, he appeared. The children stood before him, not in awe, but in need, saying, we are lost and frightened, we don't know what to do. There are so many bad things around us, so many things that are not good for us but are approved by others. We are confused and hurt, and we are fearful of the ways of the world. We cannot live as our parents want us to live, we cannot do as our teachers and church are teaching us to do. We have no one else to turn to, nowhere else to go. Help us, please.

He answered, saying, In deep sympathy with you, I am, my children. It is unfortunate, but you live in an age of unparalleled corruptness and immediacy, and learning comes to you un-filtered, and without prudence or forethought. You live in an age of commerce and individual freedoms, which often equates with greed, baseness, and a loss of responsibility. Your parents cannot shield you from all that is wrong, neither can the teacher or the church teach you to become blind to the sordid, or deaf to all that discomforts you. There are many things in place to console and reassure you, just as there are many laws to protect you; but they cannot always work in your favor, nor will they ever be plentiful or forceful enough to bring you lasting calm. Thus, it is up to you to make the best of all that you encounter.

If you have no choice but to walk in a path laden with evil, walk as if evil is to serve the higher good through you, as if it is bound to serve a better purpose in the world. It is the same with those of ill repute. Use them as if they are to give you strength. If you have no choice but to hear the voice of the profane, let it be overridden by the poetry that is within you, treat it as if it were there to make you decipher the notes of music, or there to enable you to capture the splendor of melody. If you have no choice but to feel the pulse of wickedness or the close breath of temptation, treat it as if it were in your presence to do nothing more than strengthen your resolve and steady your hand in the pursuit of that which is worthy, that which will honor your mother and your father, and give justness in an unjust world.

It is written that a child shall lead them. It must be so; it will be so, for you are the chosen ones. You are to lead by your choosing, not by the strong will of those things you have seen, heard, and felt under circumstances that were not favorable to you or your cause.

In your struggles over right and wrong and good over evil, you are to remember that you are as the clear waters, the green pastures, the sun-touched leaves, the golden meadows of swaying stalks. You are the good.

Hither and yon are you to spread your goodness; for you, my blessed children, are not only the good, you are the ever-changing winds of a brand-new day.

He was the epitome of the proverbial bug on the windshield of life.

He was also was getting close to Judgment Day, but he didn't know it. He was too busy living up to his commitment of being a scoundrel. He did it well. There was hardly a sin or crime on the books he hadn't committed, or hadn't been responsible for committing. Through chicanery and manipulations of the law by his attorneys, he did not pay a price.

He never would, it seemed.

Coming out of court after scoring another victory late one heat-oppressive day in Fort Wayne, Indiana, he was accosted by a withered old woman with a strange and haunting voice. She was deformed, and had curiously large ears. She wore her hair loosely, and her face didn't do much by way of masking torture and grief. She said to him, Your day of reckoning is at hand. She started to cackle, but then decided not to. She walked away, saying nothing else.

It was an apparition, thought he. It sometimes happens when victory is overwhelming.

As it happened, a week after the victory,
the scoundrel found himself bedridden in the
hospital. He had fallen seriously ill, and despite
the use of morphine and other sedatives, his
pain grew to be about as much as any human
could bear. He was in so much pain that he no
longer fought the idea of dying. Apparently
the decision found interest with Death, who
quietly began a bedside vigil.

As often happens with the seriously ill and
highly medicated, the man thought he was hallucinating. Still, with only minutes to go, and
hoping for redemption through a different
form of manipulation, he filled the moments in
prayer, then went to sleep. When he awoke, his
agony had increased. It was stronger than ever.
Why'n hell am I in so much pain? he groaned,
and now thinking was alone in the room.

You are in pain because of the pain you've
caused, came the strange voice, having returned

bedside. And you will be in pain for as long as you've caused pain, she added.

Answering himself, he said, What'n the hell was I praying for? And if I gotta go through this much agony, I'm glad I'm dying.

You are not dying, said she, rising from the bed to leave. It's Judgement Day, and I've just commanded that you live.

She touched him and left.

Still thinking he had been hallucinating, the man thought nothing of the touch or reply. But in that instant, he did feel that he was going to live. Better, still, he also thought he was going to overcome his pain. In fact, in the days that followed, he had begun to feel better. He started planning for his future.

On the fourth day, the withered old woman with the strange voice returned to the man's room and saw that he was packed and ready to leave the hospital. He was looking good, but he was beginning to feel a troubling new pain.

The woman gave him a sobered look. She

left without saying anything. Partway down the corridor she started to cackle, but she caught herself. She knew that it was improper to chortle or make merry until the job was completely done, and this was just a start.

The man had a long way to go. After all, he was "going to be in pain for as long as he had caused pain," after which there were the many penalties to pay, along with a host of other things; and then, for completion, the taking of the body itself — and the always tricky chore of refueling it for all eternity.

But the old woman's urge to cackle was understandable.

It often happens with all the devil's disciples when victory is so overwhelming.

And what is the secret
of your success?
Keep breathing, came the answer.
The rest is up to you.

127

It was during a slashing North Carolina rain. He had been rejected again This time, it was eating at him with a vengeance. He was never going home again. He was seated on the cold concrete at the foot of the statue, the one with the wreath around her head and a tablet and scale in her hands. She was called Justice. It was not his first time being there. The way he was feeling, it was certain to be his last. He was thinking about ending it all, and the bridge was only a block or two away. He was conscious of the statue, but not the hard rain. It was fine with the statue, she was used to people like him.

You've been rejected again, said she, looking down on him. Getting no response, she continued. How could you have expected them to accept you, when you haven't accepted yourself? Do you realize you are Truth, and that if you accept yourself as Truth, all will be well? Of course you have weaknesses, as is expected of human beings. But do you realize that if you dwell only on your weaknesses and negatives, and continue to walk with the heavy air of pessimism, as though you are programmed to fail, you will fail?

Since statues can't talk, the man thought he was in conversation with himself. I've always done the best that I could do, he said, wringing his hands. I have faults, but I am only a man.

You are wrong, said she. You are cells, corpuscles, flesh, bones, a temple of hope — much more than I or any other statue will ever be. What human isn't? But if that's all you feel you are, small wonder you are where you are. And if you feel that being a man is all that you will ever be, then this is the state of mind you will always have. That being the case, you'd be better off going to the bridge.

All I've ever asked for was a fair shot, he continued lamenting to himself.

A fair shot? she repeated. You are Earth's truth, accept it. You are hope; build on it. You have life, treasure it. You can change — *do* it.

There isn't a statue, monument, or tribute that I know of who wouldn't trade places with you or any living, breathing soul. And they would do it in a heartbeat, even in the nadir of your despair. They would give anything just to be able to breathe one time, to be able — if only for the briefest moment — to touch, to feel, to smell, to laugh, sing, dance; and maybe even to experience the greatest of all your sensations: to love. But this cannot be done. Statues can only stand as statues. Granted, some of us will stand for an eternity — something you can't do, but, in the end, we'll still be nothing more than lifeless objects. We're made of stone. But I guess none of this is of interest to you, so why bother? Maybe you're right; maybe it's best that you not go home again. So, go to the bridge. Do what you have to do. But as you take the plunge, remember what you people say: What goes around, comes around. And it might be well for you to consider this: since nobody but nobody knows anything about the hereafter, maybe it'll be your turn to be a statue. If it is, and you're given an assignment like mine, hurry to let them know you don't need a blindfold. You're already blind, and, better than any statue, you've spent a lifetime *wishing*, rather than *doing*.

Still in conversation with himself, the man said, Oh, God, how I wish I could see my way out of this. Then he stood and went home.

All that night he lay in bed, thinking. Then it dawned on him. The next morning he was up bright and early, and was ready to challenge the world. He made some appointments, then, in the bright of day, went back to the statue. Comfortable with the moment, he looked up at her and smiled. And then he left, winking and waving, and pointing knowingly at her blindfold.

Some of the people who saw him thought he was a nut.

Others who had been in his position knew he was giving thanks.

After the United States, Brazil was the greatest slave-holding nation in the new world. Things have changed since the early 1800s. It is believed, however, the weather is the same.

She was not tolerant of others; she was a first-class citizen with a second-class mind. Said she to her junior high schooler, You are young and beautiful. You have a whole life ahead of you. Do not talk to anyone such as the one who seeks to court you. He is dark-skinned, he is beneath your station. He is not your kind.

In high school, he called again. They talked, his words were kind and warm.

Do not leave this house with him. He is dark and worthless. He has no future. He will bring you nothing but harm. He is a worm, she added.

In college, they went out. The flame was still there; a courtship ensued.

Do not carry on with him. You will lose your self-respect, and the respect of others.

After college, they carried on; they became engaged.

Do not marry him. He is scum. He has kinky hair, and is not of fair skin. Your days will be filled with tears and misery.

Back home, they pledged themselves to each other. They were committed, and soon they were married.

Do not bear his children. They will be dark and inferior, and their days and nights will be filled with shame, want, and need.

They had children, and the children were reared in the surety of love. They grew to be beautiful and prosperous, and they married well, as did their children, as will their children's children, it is believed. The original two would not get to see the long line of descendents they had started, but they passed on, knowing well that, even with the best of intentions, mothers do not always give the best advice.

My Dear Son, the immigrant spoke from the Valley Inn, her restaurant there in Sherman Oaks, a well-to-do suburb of Los Angeles.

It is called a bar mitzvah. It is a rite of passage, so to speak — that of a son becoming thirteen and henceforth assuming the moral and religious duties of an adult. It has been that way for centuries in our faith, and underlying it all is the love, respect, and admiration that we have for you and for each other; and, never to be forgotten, the devotion we have to our faith. That faith — our people — and all that we stand for is being tested today as it has rarely been tested before. As Russians we are accustomed to being under siege, but, more important, as Jews we have always stood firm in the eyes of God. To a large extent, we have done so because of people like you, our youth.

As you enter the world of the adult, both your father and I, along with your beloved brother, would like nothing more than for you to enjoy the years that lie ahead, but we hold firm to the hope that you will always direct some of your energies toward serving your God, your heritage, and this, our new country. We were not born in America, but we have been welcomed as though we had been. It is not surprising; it is the American way. This is a country of ideals, of hope and freedom — all of which we ask you to treasure, and, when necessary, fight to preserve. God put us here to serve. He placed your father and me here to have you, and to guide you. We have been blessed by the results. We are grateful to Him and this country, and we are proud of you. We are prouder still of what you are to become.

In the language of our heritage, we say both *mazel tov* and *shalom*, my son. In the language of your future, we say, farewell to childhood; welcome to adulthood.

We love you dearly.

It was during the time of war. The uncle was most proud to learn that his nephew had joined the Army. In addition to serving his country, he was sure to get an education; he would see the world. He would not have to do as the Uncle had done, spend a lifetime of torture and illiteracy in the back woods of Mississippi, fighting and plowing the stubborn fields.

The letter arrived on a Wednesday.

Dear Uncle Junie,

I hoap you fine sombode to rede this leter to you. I am find and I hoap you the same. I no you mad at me for not writein. But I been so busie lateley I just could nt get aroune to it. I am a solder in the U.S. army like I said I was gone to do when I left home. So pleas don't wory about me. I am find. I hoap you will be the same. Latelly I been havieng dreams about you and all the farm and Miss Wheatly Peels and Mr. Oscell. I mist all of you. But not Mr.

Oscell. Uncle Junie | no you no ther is a war goin on. | am goin to go to it. |t is somoethin like the war you use to tel me abou. | still thinke abut the storyes you use to tel me about. | wish | coulde been in that one with you to. | am a privat firs class now. | use to be work for the majur. becase | do so good heer. | donot work for him now. | am doin somthing else impurtent. Seince we moved aroune so much | cant put where you can write tme at. But | wil keep on writein to you. | wil write much moor that | use to becaus | no how impoten it is to write to sombody you love. | have plente of time to writ befor | go to the oversees place. But like you al way say when | was a boy the army is a good plase for you to go. | am glad | come in here. Like | said a litle wile ago pleas donot try to writ to me becaus | am movein aroune so much and | am goin to go ovrsees to the war. So you can just waite for my leter to comes to you becaus | will write reglar now becaus | have time to do the writeing. Tell evebode | no that |

said hellow and be true to the lord. And dont
worre abou me.

Your loveing nepfhew.

~~Privite Nathaniel~~
Privite firs class
Nathaniel Carrol in
the Unided State Army

His letter carried the postmark: Fort
Leavenworth, Kansas. It is the home of one of
the Army's largest prisons.

— For a young soldier unable to adapt to
the rigors of the military; a stockade can be a
lonely place. But no matter where, no matter
what; always the thoughts are of home and the
family; the family and home.

Any City, Anyplace, World.

They have stepped on me,
They have trampled over my domain,
They have allowed their young
To run at large.
Long have I lain here,
In this necropolis.
I am the dead.
I am still not at rest.

140

Historic Philadelphia. Rough night in a bad hotel. Up, showered, and out, it is early morning. The sun is late; looks like it's going to be another scorcher. It doesn't make any difference to him. Handkerchief out, he is on his soapbox, his finger jabbing at the air. He is just a few feet from the Liberty Bell. It doesn't matter. Nothing or nobody is going to stop him from making his views known to the world.

America, he is saying, is full of crap. There's a certain kinda people that's tryin' to run the country like the Communists use'ta try to run the world. An' you know damn well who I'm talkin' about. An' what hurts me most is, they getting' away with it. They getting' away with ruinin' the country, an' I don't see why in hell our governmen' is lettin' 'em do it. Them bastards in the Capitol is lettin' 'em get away with any damn thing they want. We elect them peoples to represent us, then they get to Washington

an' don't do a damn thing but sit on their be-
hinds and kowtow to a bunch of low-down
good-for-nothin' ingrates that don't do a
damn thing but take free handouts from the
governmen', make babies, get drunk, smoke
dope, and bitch an' moan about what all they
ain't got. Well, they don't deserve a damn thing.
They don't deserve nothin', and that goes for
all them so-called do-gooders that's tryin' to
help 'em. All they int'rested in is stirrin' up
trouble. Th' bastards.

He thinks about it for a moment more, then
rumbles on, This country makes me sick! Absolutely sick!

— I remember him from long ago. When the
war was over and the boys came home, there
was a front-page shot of him kissing his beloved.

He was kissing the ground.

It is cold and damp in the nation's capital, but Lincoln still sits and Washington's monument still soars upward. It is past the stroke of midnight, and though all seems to be at rest, I think I hear voices echoing in the darkness...

It is not the affairs of state that make us
great, It is the people of the land;
Let us treat our poor so they want no more,
And rush not a foreign hand.

His words were not heeded, the poor were
not treated, And upset they seemed to be.
A million people walked around the land,
And sickness did they see.

Let us not think in flaw and pass a law
To aid a country afar;
Let us first school our poor so they'll know more,
A part of us they are.

They heard him not, the poor were not taught,
And unhappy they seemed to be;

A million people walked around the land,
Only darkness did they see.

Let us be fair, and exercise care
For the people of our shores;
First feed our poor so they want no more,
And then knock on distant doors.

The poor went to bed, they were not fed,
Hurt they seemed to be;
A million grains went on a ship,
And sailed across the sea.

Again we've neglected the poor and
rejected, I fear time is running out,
At least clothe the poor so they freeze no more
And allay a growing doubt.

The poor were not clothed,
And when they arose,
There was a fire in their eyes;
Buildings tumbled, great monuments crumbled
— And that's how a government dies.

And so what did the doctor say?
He said it doesn't look good.
Did you try praying?
He said he wanted cash.

Adak, Alaska; waiting to go fishing at Kuluk Bay. The "Last Frontier's" southernmost community, it has 16 miles of paved roads, one store, one school, 24 students, and 316 inhabitants, of which five are black. It has degrees of unruly appeal and a zestful bite. It's listed as a second-class city. With an accumulated snowfall of 100 inches, the temperature ranges from a bone-aching 20° to an insecure 50°. The 100-knot winds, squalls, and wind-chill factor are most inhospitable. The cold has a way of stifling conversation, but few things can be as frosty as sitting in an igloo, listening to an ill-timed observation.

Your skin is dark and your feet are flat, said one Eskimo to the other Eskimo. Surely, you must admit some kinship to the ape.

I will, my chilly friend, countered the darker Eskimo. But first, permit me the luxury of reminding you that his lips are thin and his hair is straight.

Jupiter, Florida; the cool of the evening.

The siren was not loud, but it was effective — effective enough to cause the retired suburbanite to pull his small car to the curb.

The policeman on the motorcycle pulled in back of the car. He made his approach.

On a minor violation, he usually let the offender off with a warning — particularly if the offender looked as if he came from the better part of town, and particularly if the car sported a favorable bumper sticker, such as this one did.

But the balding suburbanite's wife was a feisty one, and said she to the officer before he could open his mouth, First of all, I don't see why you're stopping us. Next, you'd do better by concentrating on some of these undesirables that's flooding our community. I don't see why you people like to pick on innocent taxpayers. It's people like us who pay your salary.

The husband sandwiched in a word. And

we pay you too damn much, if you ask me.

The policeman secured the man's driver's license, returned to his motorcycle, scratched out a ticket, and came back to the man. The wife was still steaming. Don't forget, young man, it's still us decent, law-abiding citizens who pay your salary. And we don't take this lightly. Do you know, we're retirees?

Ignoring her, the cop silently handed over the ticket for signature, then left.

Jerk, she steamed. All of 'em, a bunch of jerks. And you noticed he showed absolutely no respect at all for us retirees. Disgusting! You should've unloaded on him, Henry.

Said he: Next time, I just might do that.

It was troubling that neither of them thought about the little car's bumper sticker. It read: Support Your Local Police.

Far more chilling was the fully-loaded .45 Henry kept under the front seat.

It had been used a time or two before.

They lived in a quietly removed burg in Connecticut. There, the shades were drawn early. He would have preferred something different. Except for tinkering in the yard during the day, he enjoyed cranking up and cruising the streets at night. The later, the better.

She was cantankerous and suspicious, and thought that, as a husband, he was unfaithful, and that his love of the late-night hours more than proved her beliefs.

She did not believe that there were times when a man just wanted to be alone, to cruise a sleeping city at hours past the stroke of midnight; to see the skeletons of night ready the city for the morrow. She did not believe that at all. But that was all the husband wanted to do, and that was all he did.

It was not to his fortune. Nor was it to hers.

One night there was a crime. It was the ultimate, the most dastardly of all deeds, said the police. The city was not at peace. The city fathers demanded an arrest. It fell to the police to arrest the midnight cruiser. The wife was not surprised. Any man, thought she, and said she to the police, who was not true to the rule of marriage and would lie to his wife about wanting to be alone and come up with a most unseemly tale about roaming around "just to see a city sleep" has to be guilty of something — and it wouldn't be a surprise if it included murder. He certainly had the opportunity. And, she repeated more than once, as a husband, he certainly wasn't true to the rule of marriage.

The police believed her, the jury believed the police. And now she was alone.

One night the culprit struck again.

The midnight cruiser wanted to attend his wife's funeral, but he was denied the opportunity.

True to the rule regarding death row inmates, the authorities wouldn't allow it.

It is a long and thoughtful flight, coming back to America from Marseille, France. Situated southeast on the Mediterranean coast, it was a city that had bite, bouillabaisse, and plenty of old-world charm and provincialism. And the people were varied. From Italy, Germany, Spain, Armenia, Greece, Indochina, East and West Africa — from everywhere the immigrants came, swelling ancient streets, Vieux Port and its boat-crowded waters. Having already been to England, the Netherlands, Germany, Belgium, and Paris, and, bypassing Spain to backtrack home, you think of all that you've seen in Europe. You think about America's newness — its power; its richness. You look down on the idling clouds. Commingling thoughts send the mind drifting all the way back to that time when you thought you heard a maiden speak.

I thought I heard the maiden say: I was once a name, but I have returned to being a condition. Before becoming a name, I had been long in obscurity, and, like the perennial bridesmaid, I wanted to be centered up front, to be in a position to catch the bouquet of happiness, and, later, sip from the cup of acceptance. I felt that the clutches of need and desire had just cause to single me out. Those who knew me well said, no, it shall never be. Still, just as that perennial bridesmaid, I wanted someone to take a closer look at me. But none did, and so I became tempestuous — riotous, as some will recall. I became that way, and for one sweltering weekend, every human emotion traversed my veins and touched the nerves of millions. I had, at last, wedded recognition. But though I had, I was not accorded the glory of the bride. I was accorded none of the niceties of betrothal, nor was there a honeymoon. Still, there was an unforgettable vibrancy to the affair.

My long-sought union attracted reporters, pundits, and cameras from all over the world. I even had the concern of the President, the concern of the U.S. Senate, and Congress. Even the military was in attendance. There were firemen also. But none could outnumber the police. They were everywhere. At the time, some went so far as to say that the police had even sponsored the event. Certainly their contributions couldn't be denied. But it matters not now. What happened to me was years ago. Time has moved on. It would be nice to say I have moved with time, but I haven't. In a way, neither has anything else.

Now you stand there, searching my face. And then, strange, you say, you cannot remember my union with recognition.

You say you hardly remember me.

I understand. You're not alone. And don't feel embarrassed, dear. As I said before, I was once a name. I'm back to being a condition.

They call me Ghetto — any ghetto; any city, USA. And, almost like the far-flung places in Europe, I have not changed. I am still old-world. Of course, I never had the charm or the provincialism of Europe, but I am still old-world.

No one vacations here.

Oh, and, dear: please don't forget: In addition to claiming a number of lives? my wedding to recognition cost untold millions.

True revenge is cruel. It stems from the damnedest people, for the most peculiar reasons, and from the strangest places.

He was from the hills of Tennessee, and he fancied himself a balladeer. He loved the freewheeling life of a banjo-strumming poet. But it was not to last. He troubled a young lass in a barn one night, and her shotgun-toting father took the necessary steps to cut short his freedom.

From the honeymoon capital of the world, he wrote the father:

Dear Daddy-in-law; I'm writing to you in pain,
And I hope, sir, this letter finds you the same.
You know your daughter and I could never get along,
But you said the wedding, sir, must go on.
Oh, what a sad affair;
Oh, what a sad affair;
Oh, oh, oh, what a sad affair.

I was in tears when you drug me down
the aisle,
And when you wouldn't let me say "no" to
none of the vows,
My friends, just a-weeping, said, look'a
there—
Ain't that one real sad affair.
Oh, what a sad affair;
Oh, what a sad affair
Oh, oh, oh, what a sad affair.
Then we left you, sir, heading for our
honeymoon.
But your daughter won't be back, no time
soon.
Daddy-in-law, your daughter is now rest-
ing 'neath,
A little stone that says: Rest In Peace.
Oh, what a sad affair;
Oh, what a sad affair;
Oh, oh, oh, what a sad affair.

The dusty, oak-panelled room in the small, tucked-away Kansas township was packed. It didn't have to be. Selecting the new police chief wasn't supposed to that be much of a contest.

So the story goes, the town council had narrowed the list down to two men. One had been on the job for twenty years; the other, by way of comparison, was an upstart.

When the council got around to taking the final vote, it was the upstart whom they selected to be chief. The crowd was stunned, but the veteran policeman was outraged. He stood and blistered the air. How, in God's name, could you people do such a thing?! He was so loud and upset, his wife was yanking on his coattail, trying to get him to sit back down.

He wouldn't stop. I've got over twenty years on this department! I've given this city the best years of my life! *Twenty years!*

Doesn't twenty years experience mean anything to you people?!

Twenty years experience means a lot to us, said the eldest member of the council. But we listened to every word you said. We listened very carefully. Every day you've taken the same route to work, every day you did the same when you arrived at work. And when you left work, still you did the same. What it means is, you do not have twenty years experience. What you have is one year's experience, repeated twenty times.

It was the end of the month in one of Wisconsin's more polite suburbs. The city's budget was in trouble, and Charlie the cop hadn't reached his quota. The city wasn't happy.

Then came a speeder.

Siren blasting, sunglasses on, Charlie ran four red lights, two amber lights, one railroad crossing light, six stop signs, and two proceed-with-caution warnings. The offending vehicle dropped out of sight, but it didn't stop Charlie. He was more determined than ever. He zipped up one one-way street, zoomed down another, left tire tracks in the park and skid marks at the intersection of First and Central. He caused two Fords to collide, two other cars to kiss, and forced a truck to caress a pole. He sideswiped a Lincoln, forced a Plymouth to greet a Mustang, and sent a Volkswagen shopping through a storefront window. He interrupted a ball game, caused Mr. Bentley to suffer a stroke, Miss Cora to collapse, and

sent Mr. Leek keeling over in fright. He by-
passed a burning building, overlooked a drowning, and paid no attention to a holdup-in-
progress. By accident, Charlie sped down a
dead-end street. It was the one he had passed
earlier, but that was not important — for there
he saw the speeder, and there Charlie the cop
reached his quota.

And there Charlie made the city happy.
The city's budget would be fed, and all the
motorists in the polite little suburb could rest
easy another month.

In the old days,
they used to say:
Stop, or I'll shoot!!
Today th—

It was in a time-mellowed B.R. Smith building in downtown Ardmore, Oklahoma. Time may had mellowed the building, but it did little or nothing to advance the minds of certain people.

All during the treatment the patient had talked incessantly, and both his grammar and his state of mind were putrid. When the doctor was through, the man rose from the table, swung his legs to the floor, buttoned his stained and smelly shirt, zipped up his ill-fitting trousers, and concluded, My ol' granddaddy used to say every white man should own one. But now, you take a boy like yourself. I wouldn't mind lettin' you live next to me.

The doctor thanked him and they both returned to his diploma-heavy office. Quietly he filled out the patient's papers and handed them back to him. The man was on Medicare. But the doctor didn't say anything. He didn't have to. The black one knew that a station in life was not always a station in mind.

He had climbed the ladder of New Jersey success. From his perch, they said, he was not one to look down or back. They said that in order for him to have attained such heights in a corporate world he had to have the soul of a snake and the hide of a rhinoceros; that he would not remember nor would he care about an old never-achieving boyhood friend who was succumbing to terminal illness. But someone contacted him. His response was immediate.

What he wrote reminded one of a good man, a classy man. He reminded me of the long-time TV producer, Dean Hargrove.

My Dear Friend:

There will come a time when we all will be forced to take the full view of life. Doubtless it will be concluded that it is untimely and unfair. And while on the surface it may appear that it is, it is up to us to give thought to our very reason for being. I believe our purpose is to serve for the betterment of mankind. We have not kept in touch, but I would like to say that I have often thought of you, and that neither time, distance, nor occupation can alter the fact that I envy you. I have made money, but you have served for mankind's betterment. You may not have been heralded, applauded, properly rewarded, or held high in the public eye such as I have. But, in your own way you have achieved more. You were a public servant, and therefore you have reached something higher. More important, beyond my knowing it, beyond earthly man knowing it, God knows it. And that, my dear friend, is as much as any mortal can ever hope for.

I shall never forget you.

—The friend was pleased. He died within days of receiving the letter. He had been a sanitation worker.

Many called him a garbage man.

What he said was,
From your lips to God's ears.
What he meant was,
From God's lips to your ears.

Greetings from Cleveland, Ohio. In the 1900s it was the nation's 4th largest city. A trade center with many interests, it has always shown promise. It is disturbing to think, however, that recently the roof of a school fell in.

It was a tiny group that had gotten even tinier over the years. They were old, impoverished, and outdated. They were bearded, shoeless, and wore bell-bottoms and multicolored clothes. The women wore flat, faded flowers in their hair, and together they sat on the bank of Lake Erie in solemnity, speaking of the police and their near-death experiences.

Tell us, What is this tunnel we are being driven to? What do we make of this golden light that beckons us to the Other Side?

The robed one answered, saying, Do not be misled. You have seen neither a tunnel nor a golden light. You are in fear of being without that which has sustained you through life, and you are seeing the beginnings of your brief moments here on Earth, before the rise of the good that you have inhaled through the years. Your inhalations have caused you to rise above the hurricane, the flood, the earthquake, and all manner of disasters and man-made horrors, the central one being the most archaic of laws. And even though you are constantly being strongarmed, browbeaten, and pursued by the arm of law, and, many times, have had your gardens sprayed, disrupted and destroyed because of many judicial indiscretions, you must continue to live in recognition of the good that springs from the Earth. Let man nor law stop you. Continue planting your seeds. Continue harvesting in abundance. Inhale well; and, always and in all ways, remember to share your largesse with the Main Brother.

Pleased, and as they had done every year, they paid the Main Brother with an abundance of well-rolled joints. And as they had done every year, they lit up and made plans for the next hippie convention.

It is nocturnally quiet both inside and out, and this old house creaks without reason. It is not a comforting place to spend the night.

Good Evening. It is almost Tuesday night in Smyma, Delaware.

He had been busy going from door to door, handing out his card. He didn't get around to her house until long after darkness had fallen, and when he did, he knocked on the door quietly and respectfully. His card was in his hand. Business was not good, and he was hoping to make it better.

She was not quite as old as he, but she lived in fear of the Grim Reaper, whom she had always feared and was sure she would meet prematurely. In fact, meeting the Reaper and facing her quietus bothered her so much that there were days when she would go miles out of her way just to avoid passing the funeral home.

Worse were her nights.

Every night was a mental disaster, and sometimes she would go so far as to try to sleep standing up. Failing in that, she wouldn't sleep at all.

Normally she wouldn't have opened the door at that hour, but there was a guest upstairs, and she felt secure. She wasn't unduly disturbed at the presence of the black-suited man with the hunched back and deliberate face until he handed her the card.

She read the card; she was dead before she collapsed to the floor.

— It is said that the old should always be respected, and that the old seeking business should be encouraged. But I do believe undertakers should not be allowed to make house calls in the dead of night.

It was almost spring, yet it was snowing in Denver. Still the sun was out, paying tribute to the world. The rays glistened through muted icicles and bathed everything in a sort of benign beauty. Adding to the joy, and probably at the behest of the sun, two of the smaller rays, locked arm in arm, danced the morning away. And the clouds? The clouds were tickled pink.

It seemed a smidge irreverent at first, but, all in all, it was a good day for a funeral.

Dearly beloved, intoned the good Reverend, standing graveside with a tiny Bible in his hip pocket and a fistful of dry-eyed mourners looking on with amazing disinterest, We are gathered here today to pay homage to this dear and trusting soul who is no longer numbered among us. But though she has been called from our midst, let us not mourn for her; let us not grieve for her; for her place in our hearts and in the hearts of many is assured.

As we lower her remains into the waiting ground, let us never forget that she was a giving soul, let us recall that when all didn't go well in your home, it certainly would go well in hers. She was the bridge over troubled waters; a gateway to relief, the spreader of glad tidings; a minister of joy; a purveyor of gladness. Her doors were never closed to those in need, her house was a source of never-ending inspiration. And when all was dim in her house, she would provide merriment in the darkness. Our loss is a profound loss, because this woman was truly a servicer of mankind.

— What the good Reverend was trying to say was that the woman was the proprietress of a sin den, and he had been a lifelong customer.

Up there you wandered while you wondered. Down here, you wonder while you wander. Lots of occupations; lots of tycoons, and big-business type movers and shakers represented, but still not as crowded as it could be.

Searching for more familiar faces while leisurely strolling along the fire-lit corridors of Hades, at another section just a few feet before the big bend where the false prophets, pimps, idolaters, swindlers, martyrs, murderers, warmongers, communication trivialites, and Hollywoodians are either entombed or about to be entombed, you are surprised to notice that the hottest flames are not for the for the people who used weapons, rather they are reserved for the people who made the weapons.

—You wake up in a cold sweat, saying to yourself, Thank God I didn't have a hand in creating the Atomic bomb.

From the pages of *Say Goodnight to the Boys in Blue* it comes — repeated here because to die alone is to be alone.

Robbie was a town fixture; an unquestionable drunk. Every night he would go into Kelly's, a bar just off Main Street, and buy a half-pint of rum with money he had hustled elsewhere. It would be his last stop of the evening before ending up in a doorway on Main Street. Everyone was used to him, certainly the police. At night when Main street's post 1-A would change, the man walking the midnight shift could count on beating the chill of winter by searching the doorways and finding Robbie Smalls. Most of the time the liver-infected little ruddy-faced man with the thin and ashy hair would be shivering, not so much from the cold as from the toll that the alcohol had taken on him over the years. Robbie was a sure arrest, hence a sure way for the post 1-A man to get back to the warm confines of the police station. Sometimes the post 1-A man would be a little too aggressive in handling Robbie, but he was not one to resist. Robbie was a rummy, not a resister. It didn't matter to a policeman seeking refuge from the onslaught of the bitter cold. With the drunk in tow, the post 1-A man would call the station and a car would be dispatched to the scene. Together they would ride to the old building in silence, though the post 1-A man would already be feeling better by virtue of riding in the warm car. Filling out the record-of-arrest form at the station could have been done in a matter of minutes. If it were really cold outside, the procedure would be stretched into an hour or more. Normally, upon seeing Robbie, the desk sergeant would dig into the bottom desk drawer and give him a teaspoon of the sobering paraldehyde, and the post 1-A man would escort him back to one of the cells to sleep it off. It was another procedure that should have been over in ten or fifteen minutes — which, again, amounted to ten or fifteen minutes of additional warmth to the blue-coated and silver-shielded man who had to spend long hours trudging and fighting the long winter nights. But one night it did not happen that way. The procedure was the same, but the results were not. The midnight sergeant of the desk was a gruff and bitter man who, ironically, wasn't much larger than Robbie. But to Robbie's everlasting misfortune, the small desk sergeant had had a bad night. Robbie Smalls wouldn't get the usual teaspoon full of paraldehyde that troubled night. He got the whole bottle. Even before the post 1-A man had armed Robbie up to the desk, the sergeant saw how badly the alcoholic man was shaking, and instead of getting a spoon, he dug into the bottom drawer and sat the small bottle on the desk. Robbie was in a haze. But haze or not, he still had an alcoholic's awareness and anything in a bottle looked good to him. The weak and thin little man picked up the bottle and in one swoop drank the contents dry. It took but a second. His face contorted bitterly for a moment and then settled back into normalcy. The shaking subsided, but it didn't disappear.

The desk sergeant was not concerned. Showing no emotion, he flicked an eye on the post 1-A man and ordered him to take the drunk to the cell in back. He did, then left the station, and returned exactly three hours and fifteen minutes later. It was 0400, lunch time for the post 1-A patrolman. One of the three all-night restaurants was down the street from the street from the station, but before going to lunch, it was necessary to check with the desk. The sergeant was still there, and in checking the cells in back, found that so was Robbie Smalls. He was stretched out on the metal cot with his eyes closed. His skin had hardened into an even deeper pinkish red, and he was breathing hard for a thin man. Occasionally, he would manage a cough and the effort would send the saliva dribbling uncontrollably down his chin and the corners of his mouth. Robbie was a sick man. The post 1-A man knew it. He studied the prisoner for a bit longer, then went back up front and informed the desk of his impressions. Without even raising his head from the blotter, the desk sergeant said, Go eat, an' let me worry about the station. The post 1-A did just that. He returned to the cell twenty-one minutes later. It had not been a good lunch. Four a.m. lunches never are. But on this occasion it was particularly bad. So was Robbie Smalls' condition. His breathing was all the way down to that murky and awful-sounding bottom. The post 1-A man could feel the dry and saliva-less rattle of the esophagus. Robbie the drunk did not have far to go. He needed hospitalization in the worst way, and the policeman hurried back to the front to tell his sergeant. His words fell on deaf ears.

Said the sergeant, Get back on post. Once again, the post 1-A man did as ordered.

Zero eight hundred did not come with speed, but it came and brought with it a slow sun and post 1-A's relief man. The midnighter walked back to the station slowly. Desk sergeants usually leave about twenty minutes before the change of shifts, but, oddly, the midnight sergeant was still at the station. He was complaining because there were forms to be filled out, forms that delayed his departure.

The police physician was there also. He had to fill out forms, as well. And when the midnighter arrived he, too, had forms to fill out. It was a required police procedure. But the Post 1-A man did not have to think. The sergeant of the desk and the police physician had it all worked out.

Robbie Smalls, they said, died of natural causes.

He was going to write the great American novel, and he very well could have. He had seen the world. He was dashing, and had a tan that was so deep it was almost golden. He spoke eloquently, dressed splendidly, and was a whiz in court. He had been the high-powered lead attorney for the tobacco conglomerate, and had scored any number of victories, but his last case was a stunner. He had saved them billions of dollars, and had been handsomely rewarded. Now he had more money than he knew what to do with, and so he decided to live the high life. The globe became his oyster again, and there was hardly a night that went by when he didn't have a model of luscious proportions on his arm or in his bed. He had not one but four limousines, one for each direction, he liked to say. He acquired a private jet, and a yacht large enough to rival any in the harbor.

He was going to write the great American novel on the big boat, but he got an urgent call from another tobacco company. His services were desperately needed. At first he declined to accept the case, but, in thinking it over, the challenge was too great to pass on. The company and its executives were being sued by several states and he didn't think it was a fair fight, plus, being a smoker, although he never had to buy a cigarette or cigar, he believed that it was purely unconstitutional for a tobacco manufacturer to be held liable for something a person did and enjoyed through their own volition, and it was no worse than alcohol consumption or eating certain processed food. Of course it didn't hurt, either, that the tobacco company was offering him everything short of the moon for his services.

He took the case, assembled a battery of attorneys, marched into court and scored a victory with lightning speed. He and his team were nothing short of superb, and the tobacco company couldn't shovel enough money his way. He was drowning in riches.

On the road again, and delaying work on the book for a while longer, he became a fixture at the casino tables. Then the bug of world-wide travel and international beauties bit at him again. And again he was off to circle the globe, thinking that it would be a nice idea to include a chapter or two in the book about cruising the high seas, then toss in a few tidbits about dining in Paris, tasting the nightlife in Monte Carlo, seeing the sights in Rome, skiing the Alps, attending the bullfights in Spain, sunning in the Caribbean, touring Chicago, walking the sidewalks of New York, eating caviar and foie gras in San Francisco, and drinking Dom Perignon from a glass slipper in Beverly Hills.

He did all those things and more, but now it was time to settle down and write, even turning down a call from another tobacco company.

It was an offer not to be believed — and being placed on the firm's board with an open-end check and unlimited stock options were only inducements. But this time, nothing was going to stop him from sitting on his yacht and tackling writing. At first the book was going to be a work of fiction, but, he thought, his life had been stronger than fiction. That was the route to take. And take it he did.

He did well for the first few weeks. The thoughts came fast and orderly, and he got as far as sketching out the first few chapters, then suddenly he couldn't go any further. It was particularly troubling, because he had pushed writing about the high life aside, and was at the point of explaining his courtroom strategies.

The next chapters were going to be just as illuminating. They were going to be about inherent rights, and how the tobacco companies should never lose a case, and that no company — no executive of a tobacco company — deliberately sets out to harm or cause injury to anyone. What they provided enhanced pleasure, soothed nerves, and acted as a stimulus to the brain. But he would never get the points across, because he fell ill and had to be hospitalized.

He underwent a number of surgeries, with the doctors doing their best. But, like his wealth, their best wasn't good enough, and so on a blustery Wednesday morning he was brought back to his boat and placed in the stateroom. He was there for a day, his fragmented mind darting in and out, occasionally touching on his innumerable victories in court. He wasn't quite so proud of them now, but it was too late. By morning he was gone. He had succumbed to the twin illnesses of emphysema and lung cancer.

His funeral was to be held within days. In the meantime, his aides spent time rounding up pallbearers. The first call went to a loyal and long-standing friend, who happened to be president and CEO of the largest of the tobacco giants. The exec was remorseful but talkative until the aide told him the cause of death. Then the man fell silent. The aide picked it up: Can we list your name as a pallbearer, sir?

If you do, said the chief exec, I'll sue you and the corpse.

It soared. It looked as if it would best the clouds and scrape the sky. It was a day of searing beauty. She was at the very top of the much-praised building, looking straight ahead.

She was transfixed. One foot was teetering on the ledge, the other was soon to follow.

A moment more, and it would be all over.

She had no choice, she felt.

She was convinced that life had been unfair. Business was bad, socially things were unendurable, and domestically everything around her was in irredeemable disarray. And she was lonely. All through life she had been lonely. All through life she felt as if she had made bad choices, feeling that she had selected the wrong mate, the wrong friends, the wrong road; the wrong everything. Life was unbearable.

As she moved the second foot into a position, enabling her to jump, it said to her, I am doing as you wish, but, I pray you, m'lady, think of the many years that I and my companion foot have served you. We have always done as you have commanded. Some of the ways have been wrong and questionable, and they have been without reward or pleasure, but the ways were not ours to question, and never were they our footprints. They have always been yours. Is it right, then, that all is to end in this fashion? Is it right that this is the manner of thanks we get? Joining in were the legs. The foot is altogether right with the questions, they said. From infancy to this day, we have carried you to wherever you have directed us to go, and, like the foot, many were the times when we knew you were wrong and misdirected, yet we went. We went because our sole purpose in life has been to serve you, and only you, and to serve you without question or reservation. It is known that you have been growing ever more impatient and distraught, and that even in your hours beyond midnight long have you lain awake, murmuring and thinking of what is not fair. Yet in your misery and unneeded loneliness, you wish to terminate us in a fashion that is not fair, right, nor godly. Then the torso spoke. Aye, it said. I cannot help but be in full agreement with the legs and feet. What you seek goes beyond unfairness. It is beneath dignity. It is selfish and unworthy of respect. It will not decently preserve your memory, nor will it ever show appreciation for those things that have served you for a lifetime. I ask you, what if we had done what you seek to do? — and this I ask in the name of all that is within me. I ask on behalf of the liver, the lungs, the spleen, the kidneys, the bladder, the appendix, the colon, the uterus; I ask in the name of the blood — and for the mightiest among us, the heart and all its rhythms; I ask even for things yet to be defined, such as the soul and spirit. We are in concert, and we all say that many have been the times when we have been ill and upset and have wallowed in dismay and distress because of your consumption and your choosing. Thanks to medicines, pills, and our natural regenerative powers, we have always recovered, and we have always been here to serve you, and we have done so with undiminished loyalty and devotion. And to prove it, if there need be proof, we have even brought you to this point — the point of your impending demise. And ours. Concurring were the arms. They spoke, then gave way to the shoulders and neck, who spoke at length and in heartfelt earnestness, then deferred, leaving the concluding remarks to the head. It yielded and summoned the brain.

With great and bone-chilling detail, the lofty organ spoke softly and painted a gruesome picture of a body lying splattered on the streets below. Bones and tissue were laid bare, fecal matter was seen, and the blood flowed from the intestines as if there were no end. From the witnesses, tears welled from the eyes of both young and old, and even the most hardened of men recoiled in repulsion and horror.

The brain then spoke of that which could not be seen — the toll that an act of utter selfishness would have upon others; and of the rewards of patience; and of hope and promise; and of the uncertainty of the hereafter, saying clearly that dying has never proven itself to be better than living. And it never will. Then, finally, the most revered of all the organs said, I entreat you to hold on, as matters will get better. They always do. But if you insist, I and my companions will go where you will yourself to go, just as we have done all through our lifetime together. We will meet our end, as you are determined to meet yours. In this hour of self-selected tragedy — and surely one that does not have to be— I say to you, farewell, m'lady; it has been nice knowing you... as we knew you.

It didn't take long. The woman climbed down from the ledge, and with help from both her surface and all that was deep within, she resumed her career, hence a renewed life.

She was a builder. She has been building beautiful buildings ever since — some as tall as the one she had been standing on.

It dealt with lost loves, poetic justice and the moral rot of slavery, they said. They said it was stunning, "Faulkneresque"; powerful; subtle and richly textured; that it had wit and heart.

Apparently she didn't think so, and what she thought mattered. She was the talk-show powerhouse — a guru; the book-selling potentate. In the jargon of the trade, she could "make 'em or break 'em." America read what she read, and like a three-hankie movie, she loved stories with heart. Black men, it was felt, didn't write 'em that way. Few, if any, would get her endorsement.

It was a novel about a six-year-old, curly-haired black boy reared on the other side of slavery, deep in the back woods of North Carolina. Born on the plantation, he lived in a shanty and had nothing and no one to play with, except the land, the creek, and cornstalks. To aid his imagination, he would lie by the creek, cross his spindly legs, plant his eyes upwards, and get lost in the soft billowing clouds. That would last until his beloved uncle came home from the fields.

The uncle was a leathered old black field hand and was burdened with a hump on his back. He was so dutiful that he wouldn't ride the plantation wagon back to the shanty; he would trail the mule. The boy would hear them approaching and would race the winds to escort them back home.

After the mule was unhitched and settled, the rusted old uncle would silently prepare the nightly meal of fatback and molasses. The two of them would eat off the tin plates, then settle on the front porch. Along with the frogs and crickets, they would rear back in comfort until Mr. Archy, the bossman, came.

Mr. Archy owned the plantation, but he was a mind-troubled Scotsman, and the one thing he didn't like was the little boy. It was all right with the little boy. He loved the old white man — not quite as much as he loved his uncle —

but he still loved him, and even after receiving
his nightly tongue lashing — for reasons he
never understood — the love held firm.

It was the same when he went to bed.

Before drifting off, the boy would think
of the man and another love in his life, whom he
had seen only once. Her name was Sweet Elsie
Pratt. She was a motherly but huge woman with
glistening black skin and a roaring voice. And
even though she went away, she made an impres-
sion on his heart that would last forever.

The days grew long around the plantation,
and it appeared that nothing would ever
change. But one day, out of pure hatred and
spite, a handful of feebleminded ne'er-do-
wellers from nearby Red Springs decided that
they wanted the plantation and all the land
around it. They were the North Carolina
"weeds" and it was decided that the only way
they could get the land was by killing the plantation owner and his humpbacked field hand.

A terrible and inopportune killing, it was

done on the night when the plantation owner and his field hand had made peace with each other, and, in their revelry, had spent hours talking to the boy about how they had "seen the light.

They talked about God that night. They talked about the love of the land, and the bright days that lay ahead for the boy; they talked about his need to learn how to read and write, and the importance of him learning history — and the history of his people — and the contributions he could make, not only to North Carolina, but to the world as a whole; they talked about honor and decency, and that he was sure to meet wrongdoers — *weeds*, they called them — and that, because of who he was, the "weeds," and others, would try to take things away from him, but that at all costs, he was to use the mind; that he would know how to deal with the "weeds of life," even if it meant he had to kill them with kindness.

They talked about those things and more,

with the old black telling the boy that the only
thing he wanted in life was to see his name
spelled out on a piece of paper. This, the boy
could do for him one day. As a former slave, he
wouldn't be able to read what was written, but
at least he could see it. A letter would be nice,
but just to see his name written on a piece of
paper would do.

But that would never happen, and even
though the boy escaped that dreadful, mur-
derous night, in a sense the "weeds" had killed
him too. He never grew to be what he should
have been. But years later, when he returned
and avenged the death of his two beloveds, he
brought with him three tombstones and an envelope. In the envelope was a letter. It read:

Dear Uncle Benny:
  I can now write. And I am writing to tell you
that I met with them, the weeds who took your
life, and Mr. Archy's life.
  Before they died, I told them a tale that

was dear long ago. I told them about you; about us. I spoke to them, too, about freedom and purity; innocence lost and promises unfulfilled. But mostly, Uncle Benny, I told them about a time and a place where once there was row upon row of sky-nodding corn; where once one raced the fields and chased the winds and embraced all the joys of living; where once the clouds, like the roads to the imagination, were free and clean and pillowy — and all the coming days of my yesteryears were to be filled with hope, magic, and promise. Those days were never to be, Uncle Benny. We were all shortened by a cruel and uncalled-for wickedness.

But the wickedness of a cruel and heartless people could not take away everything. They could not take away that which I will always remember, nor could they dim the memory of three people I will always love; always cherish.

'Bye, sir.

And good-bye to you, Mr. Archy. And thank you, sir. Thank you. Oh, and Mr. Archy?

I hope you forgive me if I say that over the years
I've been too disturbed to use all of my mind.
But, sir, there was a special occasion. I gussied
up, and I think I was clever. I did my best. At
least I tried to, and I know I've made a contribution to North Carolina. The Red Springs
weeds are all gone now. And they were killed
with kindness.

Sweet Elsie Pratt, I did not know you well.
But I knew you enough to love you. Rest well.
All of you, rest well. I will see you soon.

On the subject of Hollywood, the dream capital of the world, the American playright Wilson Mizner (1876-1933) said, It is a trip through a sewer in a glass bottom boat.

With all due respect to Mr. Mizner, as you end your visit on the studio lot, you don't think of the boat. You think of who rows the boat.

He was a small man, but a giant in the industry. He was no longer merely a director and producer of note, he was legendary; the auteur of autuers. His films had long since exceeded the billion-dollar mark and, not that he needed to, as he was the head of his own production company, he could get any project that he wanted "greenlighted." One recommendation — one word — from him to any studio, mogul, or maven in town and the deal was done, no questions asked. He was the icon, the all-time boxoffice champ, the god of profits — and to sweeten the proverbial pot, in a world of megalomaniacs and back-stabbing wheeler-dealers, he enjoyed a solid reputation. To all intent and purposes, he was beyond reproach. He didn't "make the rounds," his films were moralistic, he was politically in the loop, and he was a humanitarian. A *concerned* humanitarian

When he was younger, he was just as clean.

He had a friend back then. They spent time together. They wrote together, and often talked about what they would do once they had "made it" in the tough and oppressively incestuous world of Hollywood. They knew they would succeed in the business; they were too talented not to. And even if only one of them did, it was for certain they would not lose touch with each other. They admired each other; they respected each other's talents even if the industry would not. They were *friends*. So friendly were they that when they parted from the studio lot after a day of writing, one would say to the other: Have a nice day.

Or something to that effect.

As it happened, the industry did not necessarily appreciate the friend's talents, and while he didn't exactly stutter-step into oblivion, he never came anywhere close to achieving the success that the little god had. None could. He was too stratospheric. But that was all right. The boxoffice champ was his friend and he knew that if ever he needed him, he would be there — after all, it need not be repeated, they were *friends;* they admired each other, respected each other's talents, and upon parting, one of them would always manage to say to the other: Have a nice day.

Or something to that effect.

As the icon continued his assault on boxoffice history and zoomed even higher into the stratosphere, came the day when the friend wanted someone — anyone — to greenlight a lone, ultra low-budget project he had spent years developing. He had mortgaged his house to get it to a certain point. But he could go no further. Matters were critical. He didn't want to be bothersome, but out of desperation he called his old friend — the boxoffice champ, the icon, the concerned humanitarian — the one who was so all-powerful now that even a nod of the head meant that a deal was done, no questions asked. It took a few years — about five, according to the calendar — as the icon was busy, but the friend, who by now had lost virtually everything, finally got an appointment.

He arrived early at the nicely nestled complex and, after clearing security, he was courteously ushered upstairs and into the icon's eye-catching office. Quick to be noticed, however, was that the carefree air that they used to share was no more. Here, security was tight, the atmosphere was rich but anxious, and the awards, honors, and certificates of achievements were everywhere. It was something to behold; intimidating, in a way. But it was to be an amiable meeting, with the two old friends greeting each other warmly, then settling back on the plushly comfortable sofa to spend time "catching up," and devoting time chitchatting about what used to be, and how much things had changed through the years. Squirming and anxious to sandwich in a word about his pressing needs, the visitor agreed that things had changed.

They had changed too much.

The visitor was thinking exactly the same when he left. For when he left the well-heeled office nestled in the all-powerful surroundings, he left empty-handed. Save for the chitchat, he didn't get a thing. And judging from the way the icon had danced, hemmed, hawed, and bemoaned his circumstances, he wouldn't get a thing. Not then. Not now. Not ever. He would not even get a recommendation.

But at least one thing hadn't changed. Escorting the head-hanging friend who had lost everything out the door, the little god — the billionaire — the boxoffice champ — the icon — the auteur of auteurs — the concerned humanitarian did remember one thing. He remembered to say, Have a nice day.

Or something to that effect.

So foul and fair a day I have not seen.

— Wm. Shakespeare,
Macbeth 1:3

He had the voice to speak of many things. And he often did. He had the qualifications to do so. In real life he had been a soldier, a fireman, a policeman, a television star. As a soldier in war, he had been shot in the abdomen and hit with a hand grenade. As a policeman, he had been involved in a questionable shooting. He had produced music, been an award-winning novelist, met the President, lectured at schools, and been praised for his speeches.

Best known for what he had done in reel life — in Hollywood's television and films — he had portrayed characters of all sorts. He did not, as the saying goes, always stick to the script, nor was he always focused. But he was convincing, so much so that a priest had asked him to submit his name for Emmy award consideration. Another time, after playing the "bad guy" on TV, a terrified woman saw him in a restaurant one evening and called the police.

After a long career, he retired to write novels. Creatively he did well. His books were far-ranging and highly praised, but in the crudely segregated and oppressively monopolistic world of selling books, none cracked the bestseller lists. Being an author, he came to learn, was not about the art of writing, but rather the art of the deal.

Then came the day when he was asked to return to the field of acting. The producer was reputed to be top-flight, and the role was to be the role of roles — that of a US Supreme Court justice. And although the platform was only in the make-believe world of television, still, from the great bench, he thought he would be able to say things that needed to be said, and, combined with the clear voice of experience, it would give added meaning to his people — indeed, to all the people in TV land desirous of eavesdropping on one of the single most significant entities of the American government. There would be light for the people; lessons for the children — something, colloquially speaking, to hang your hat on.

From the commendably beautiful set — from the long curved bench of solid oak — from the nine black-robed justices sitting in the big black, high-backed chairs that were fronted by the thick, red velvet curtains that looked so imperial by the flanking columns of imposing marble, it was thought there would be make-believe explorations and rulings that could enlighten the course of the nation; words that could heal and guide.

The task from the big make-believe bench could be so challenging, so daunting that his voice, in concert with the other voices, and often spoken of as a forceful voice, and his writings, often spoken of as powerful writing, would pale by comparison.

But reel life does not necessarily reflect the hope of real life, nor is it a mandate for truth.

When the program made its debut, there were but few words of wisdom from the make-believe bench, no real insights regarding the laws of the land—nothing to hang your hat on.

It was a potential denied.

The vehicle leaned heavily on pedestrianism, and it seemed only as an afterthought did they include him in the offering. But even in doing that, they went back to the images of yesteryear, most times not allowing him to speak.

Then when they did allow him to say something, save for one time, he said nothing.

— So foul and fair a day I have not seen, said the Bard.

One is forced to wonder what the Bard would have said had he had to deal with the banalities and color of American television.

Memorial Day. The Arlington National Cemetery. The awesome price of liberty. You recall a speech you gave to the unheralded. They were the military recruiters, a most important group, but none could be more important or noble than the men and women buried here — and in the Arlingtons across the globe.

In delivering the speech, it is their honor and their cause that remained uppermost in mind.

Eighty-five years ago, this nation and its allies were ending a war that was said to be the war to end all wars. It was World War 1. As history has shown, that sentiment of 1918 was not to be. Wars, in one form or another, have come and gone, and today we have taken the initial steps toward yet another world conflict, this one born out of a treachery that even the most cynical of us would have never thought possible. It is incredible to think that this new century has brought about a destruction that has doubled Pearl Harbor in immensity. Defenseless men, women, and children were the targets on September 11th, 2001, and, in a sense, so was the name of religion.

What occurred on that morning was a pure abomination, beyond words, really; and whether we wish to admit it or not, a way of life has forever changed. The attack on our two cities, our people, our symbols, and leaving untold thousands of children without at least one parent, did do one thing, however. It reawakened something in us that Admiral Isoroku Yamamoto has been credited with saying. The admiral was the commander of the Japanese fleet in the Pacific, and after bombing Pearl Harbor on the morning of December, 7th, 1941, he was supposed to have said: I am afraid we have awakened a sleeping giant and filled it with a terrible resolve.

If those indeed were the admiral's words, he was right. But now that we, as a nation, have been awakened again, it would be well to say that we have learned our lesson well, and never again will we be as negligent; as vulnerable. It would be of interest to say such a thing, but hardly judicious. For as powerful as we are as a nation, we cannot take lasting comfort in our response to that tragedy of September 11th, nor the ones that preceded it; nor can we, with all of our might and resources, reach back to the old World War I refrain and say that our full response will have even the makings of a war to end all wars. It is a cruel world that we live in today; a far smaller world than that of 1918, and technology has gone a long way toward elevating barbarity and pinpointing man's in-humanity to man. Knowing humankind's bent for evil; knowing mankind's outright failure to embrace the simple tenets of world peace and brotherhood, the Bible has long warned us that there will be war and rumors of war.

And so, my friends, that brings me to those who serve, those who have served, and those who will serve this nation in peace and in war.

It brings me to you. A short while ago you were
not in the forefront of the nation's conscious-
ness. But today you are. And what you do today will forever enable you to do as I have done
— as so many, many others have done — and that
is to be able to look back on times like these and
say: This great nation was in trouble, and I was
there to serve. It will not matter what you have
gone on to do afterward, serving your country
in a time of need will always be foremost amongst
your achievements. It will not matter whether
you've spent your time doing something you
deem menial, or find yourself weighted down with
the responsibilities of command, or end your
time in service without battlefield awards or com-
mendation, the most important thing is — the
most salient thing is — you are in uniform and
you are here to serve. The heat of today's ter-
ror will inevitably recede. We will overcome as a
people; we will persevere to even greater heights
as a nation. Flawed though we are, we are much
too committed and the enemy is much too mis-

guided for it to be any other way.

But memories will fade, the flag-waving patriotism that is so prevalent in our streets today will go away, and, in a more serious consequence, I am afraid that you in the military will resort to being under-appreciated in some quarters, and, since we are a democracy, bound to hear voices of doubt, some even enslaved by scorn. But without the military — without what you do — there would be no voices, no allowable dissent, no tolerance for scorn. There would be no democracy...no America. I say to you, if ever that were to be the case, all mankind will have suffered. Imagine, if you will, a world without the United States of America.

History will show your cause is a just cause, and, closer to the core, these are the days that you will look back upon with a pride that will never die. And, I hope, so will a reawakened nation.

Thank you for being here.

Thank you for doing all that you do.

The following account is written for the record. It is to benefit— and is dedicated to— two men. Two heroes. American heroes. One is dead; the other has my lifelong gratitude.

I had been on the front in Korea for about six months, after serving a two and one-half year stint in occupied Japan. At the time it was my second enlistment in the Army. It had just become integrated, and I was serving with King Company, 9th Infantry Regiment, 2nd Infantry Division. There were but a few blacks in the company. But race was not an issue. Survival was.

We had been under heavy attack by the Chinese forces for about a week. Somehow, before retreating earlier on the morning of August 13, 1952, one of our men was captured and was taken back to the Chinese lines. He was stripped naked and his body was tied spread-eagle on the side of the forward side of a mountain, where, with the use of binocu-

lars, his white skin could be clearly seen against
the dark, shell-stripped side of the mountain. It
was a cruel sight. Our C.O. made the decision that a patrol would be formed to rescue
the body. Along with about 13 others, I vol-
unteered and agreed to serve as point-man.
The officer in charge of the detail was 1st Lt.
Henry A. Schenks. From New York, he was a
somewhat big, reddish, Germanic-looking man
with a thick mustache.

We left our lines under a bright moon, and
stealthily walked for almost an hour. Then,
passing a field of weeds, before we got to the
base of the mountain where the body was, we
were attacked.

We had walked into an ambush.

We had no idea how many enemy troops we
had encountered, but judging from the amount
of firepower coming our way, we had to've been
outnumbered. Grenade and mine explosions,
rifle and machine gun fire came from everywhere.
Our response was quick. But it was the incred-

ible courage of Lt. Schenks who set the tone.
He was a few yards away from my left front, on
his belly; under a bright moon, seeking no cover,
mouthing indistinguishables, and firing as much
as one man could fire.

With the detail exposed, I believe the Lieutenant was deliberately trying to draw fire to
himself. I have no way of knowing how many of
the enemy he took down with him; I have no
idea as to how many of the enemy we took down
collectively, but I believe the count was high,
and it is for certain the Lieutenant got more
than his share. What he did went beyond the
call of duty. No one that I know of could match
his courage.

As with others, I was hit, and after going
down with what would later be proven to be a
superficial wound in my left thigh, I continued
to fire, as did the enemy, and as did Schenks
and the few remaining members of the patrol
who hadn't been killed or disabled.

The exchange of fire continued, then it felt

like a twig had penetrated my bulletproof vest.
I had been hit again. I remember moving to my
right; and there was another explosion. The
next thing I knew I awoke to the sounds of fad-
ing Chinese voices. But I wasn't sure. Other
than feeling thirsty and weak, I wasn't sure of
anything, and it was only when the voices trailed
off that I became mindful of what had taken
place. Then it became apparent no one else
on the patrol had survived.

All became still, then black again.

It was around dawn when I awoke and heard
a drip-dripping sound. I soon realized I was in
something like a creek. It was rimmed with brush
and an eerie phosphorescence. There was a
terrible stench, and I beganhaving a thudding
stomachache that was accompanied by a
strange lead-like taste in my mouth. I became
thirsty again, and as I moved to cup my hands
to scoop a handful of water, the fingers of my
left hand became entangled in my fatigue
jacket. The dripping sound became faster and

more distinct. Looking for my weapon, I realized my carbine was gone, but I still had my .45 and two hand grenades hanging from my vest.

I rose to my knees and soon realized there were holes in my jacket, and that my left hand was covering an abdominal wound. Sweating and fearing panic, I refused to look down, or even try to determine the seriousness of the wound. I concentrated on trying to take a drink of water.

I noticed that the ache wasn't all that severe, until I tried to lean down. That's when I knew something must have been lodged in the stomach. I was too thirsty to worry about it, and proceeded to drink a few scoops of water with my right hand, then made the decision to move.

Once on dry ground, and heading in the direction opposite of where the Chinese had departed, I was challenged by an American voice. It was barely above a murmur. I said something in return, and quietly, from a thick row of brush, a soldier's form appeared, repeating over and over again, Please don't tell. Please don't tell. Please don't tell. At the time, I had no idea what he was talking about. When he got closer, I could tell by his voice that we were about the same age, 22. He lit a cigarette, and I could see that he was Nordic looking; sandy-haired, thin featured, and disheveled.

Holding the match and looking at my abdominal area, he said, You're hurt! Oh, my God, lookit your stomach!" I remember saying something like, Shut up, don't say that!

Still talking, and overlooking what I had said, he dropped his weapon, and rushed to help me. Laying me down, he discovered I was also wounded in the leg. He spent the next few minutes trying to work on both wounds, but with my stomach being as bad as it was, there wasn't much he could do. Also I refused to move my hand, fearing that if I did, I'd lose something in the gut. He helped me to my feet, and dragging me along with my free arm slung around his neck, we moved as far away from the area as we could. He found a safe spot, and we remained hidden until dawn.

Later on, when the sun came out, I couldn't move the hand because the blood had dried the hand to the skin, but we worked on it, and remained hidden on the edge of field for awhile longer, smoking and talking. During the time, he told me about how he had "bugged out" when the firing had started, and that he had found a safe spot, where he stayed until he saw me. No one else on the patrol survived, he said. And he was very sorry for what he had done.

I understood.

With full daylight coming, he decided we should move, since we were still deep in enemy territory. It was then that I discovered my other leg was hurt. Now, with both legs being injured, and my left thigh hurting more, and the foreign object in my stomach digging deeper into my intestines, the pain wouldn't allow him to carry me in a normal way. I wondered what he was going to do. Then it occurred to me that the best thing for him would be to leave me. That's when I made the decision I would either shoot him or lob a grenade at him. After that, I'd shoot myself. It was a thought that would occur several times throughout the day. The reason being, we were still in enemy territory, and I never wanted to be taken as a POW. And even had it not been a long-held thought — and one that had been drilled into the head of anyone who had been trained by the all-black 24th Infantry, as I had been three years earlier — there was no way I could survive as a POW.

But he did his best, alternately carrying me in several positions as we moved on. We would stop every now and then for rest and a cigarette, and even though we both knew that with a serious abdominal wound, I shouldn't be eating or drinking anything, we shared water from both canteens along with his C-ration crackers and candy he had stuffed in his pockets before going on patrol.

Back on our feet again, and getting me to somehow hang on, again we crept and struggled along brush, rocks and trees for as long as we could. Then later, when we moved out into another open field, we were spotted by either the Chinese or North Koreans from another mountain position.

Out of rifle range, they threw artillery and mortar shells at us. But with all credit due to this incredibly dedicated man — scrambling and dragging me to cover and safety — once again we pulled through.

Later we made it to something like a river. There he had the most difficult chore of all. How to get both of us across was the problem. Undoubtedly, the Chinese or North Koreans were going to send a patrol after us, and so there was no time to lose. He sat me down and started pacing. This time, I thought sure he was going to leave me, and so, when his back was turned, I thought about shooting him again. I was sure the patrol was coming, and I was not going to be taken prisoner.

Not knowing what I was thinking, his eyes

on the water, he hurried off, went up and down, studying the water's edge. Then after going farther away — and out of pistol range — he came rushing back. He had found some boulders and rocks; he had found a way that looked suitable to cross.

Minutes later we were in the water, and nobody short of God can explain how he got me to the rocks, let alone to the other side of the river.

After crossing and resting up a bit, and futilely trying to light soaked cigarettes with wet matches, we were off again, trying to find our lines.

Later in the day, and after getting lost several more times, we made it to a hilly area that seemed familiar. He found a ditch, laid me in it, and made some noise to attract attention to himself. It didn't work. The response came in the form of a barrage of unfriendly fire.

My pain at this point had become unbearable and I passed out again. I awoke because he was shaking and slapping me. He was excited. We were at the foot of another hill, and he thought he saw an American soldier on the ridgeline. This time we wouldn't go into protective cover. First, there was no place to hide, and even had there been, he was too exhausted to carry on. Fully exposed, and as if he didn't care if he were shot or not, he laid me down, stood and hollered as loud as he could: "Help! Help! We're Americans!"

I faintly recall seeing a detail of our troops, scurrying down the hill with a litter, and when the medic got to me, he looked at my condition and shook his head as if to say there was no way I was supposed to be alive.

I was secured to the litter, and we headed up hill. The footing was bad, but I had no cause to worry. Struggling with the litter-bearers was the man who had struggled with me all along, still going beyond the call of duty.

After we reached the top, he said a few words, then waved good-bye.

It was the last I saw of him.

— I was first operated on at the Forward Aid Station, then was flown back to Japan for the second operation.

I had been wounded in both thighs, the spleen, and liver, but my greatest fear was that I would never be able walk upright again. I was assured by the doctors that the thigh wounds were essentially superficial and that the thick stitches in my abdomen would be removed, and, in time, I would be walking normally. After another operation, I was given a souvenir. It was a shell fragment, about a 4-inch piece of jagged metal. It had removed from my stomach. For whatever reason, the bullet was never removed.

With a "million-dollar" wound I was eligible for repatriation, but I declined. I had been trained by the all-black 24th Infantry, an outfit that did not believe in withdrawing until the job was done. Then, too, hoping for a "battlefield commission," and — as I do to this day — wanting to find the fellow who had saved me, I chose to leave the hospital in Japan and return to the front lines in Korea.

When I returned some months later, I didn't last a night. I was a mental wreck. Combat had taken its toll. I was fearful of the dark, I was afraid to stay in the bunker, and by morning, I was literally shaking like a leaf. All night, it seemed, the shell-blasted trees and stumps had started moving, and I found myself firing at an imaginary enemy.

By midday, orders were cut for me to return home. I was not in any condition to find the man who had saved me. I never got his name.

I should have gained some measure of satisfaction from a letter I received from US Senator Robert C. Hendrickson. In part it read: I have just learned from the Department of Defense of the heroic contribution you have made in foreign fields, that liberty and justice may continue in this great land of ours..." — words that should have been delivered to the man who saved me. But bearing in mind what

the Senator had to say, it is of significance to
note that, in leaving Seattle, Washington, en
route to my home in New Jersey, our chartered
plane was loaded with an interracial group of
combat veterans, some still suffering from their
wounds. In my case — and still with the bullet
lodged between the ribs — I was now entering
the first stages of tuberculosis, caused by the
polluted water I had drunk with a lacerated liver.

Because of a blinding snow storm, our
plane was forced down in Butte, Montana.
One plane had already gone down the day
before, killing 37 men. The Army, in finding us
a place to stay in Butte, selected a hotel in the
center of town. Fully uniformed, we entered the
lobby with duffle bags, bandages, and chests
dotted with medals.

The officer in charge went to the hotel
clerk to sign us in. But the clerk wouldn't allow
it. Even after being told again and again who
we were, from where we had come, and the circumstances of our arrival, still the clerk wouldn't

allow it. He said to the officer: The white fellows can stay here, but the colored one's can't.
And the colored ones didn't.

James McEachin

Postscript

I have not found the courageous man with the pale, Nordic look who, over and over, did so much to save my life. After all he went through, I often wonder what he would have thought of the hotel clerk in Butte, Montana.

I am grateful to say, though, that on Thursday, April 18, 2002, after fifty years of wanting to get in touch with the Lieutenant's heirs — or anyone — to inform them of his heroic actions on that night of August 13, 1952, I finally found someone who knew him. His name is Col. Joe Ferko. A resident of Lancaster, Pennsylvania, he served with the Lieutenant in the same unit. They had been friends.

The Colonel tells me that a search and res-

cue team was dispatched the day after the engagement to get a disposition on the patrol. No bodies were found. The team did find one combat boot, however. In it was a serial number.

The boot belonged to 1ˢᵗ Lieutenant Henry A. Schenks.

Email. Date 7/1/2002. 10:48:00 AM Pacific Standard Time.

1952-A-Lt Schenks was assigned to "K" Co. 9th Regt 2nd Division and was captured by the north Koreans and Chinese. He was captured and strungup on a barbed wire fence. I can still remember this day.

Earl Wayne Ceder

May 4, 2002. Phoenix, Arizona. A speech to the veterans.

In a world saturated with trouble, it is an honor to be here to say something to — and on behalf of — the Korean War veteran. I'd like to thank the U.S. Department of Defense's Korean War Commemoration Committee and the Arizona Department of Veterans' Services for the invitation.

— Now, then, war is unquestionably a filthy business. It is a life-taking business, and, as evidenced by the war-inducing tragedy of this past September 11th, war is initiated by humankind's worst impulses. Those impulses must be dealt with. To do so requires resolve and sacrifice. If this country's ideals and principles are to stand, they will do so only on the firm foundation of resolve and sacrifice. And that is why you, the Korean War veteran, will always have reason to hold your head high.

In a war that was so obscure it is still called by some "the forgotten war," in a war that is still so undervalued that its three-year commemoration period, hosted by our own government, has gone largely unnoticed by the national media and the people — still, veterans, you were there, willing to sacrifice all.

Overshadowed by the enormity of World War II, and the troubling complacency that followed, some will always refer to this nation's involvement in Korea as a police action; others will always refer to it as the Korean conflict. Let them call it what they may: My fellow veterans, you went to war. With the questionable count of 36,568 young Americans dead on the field of battle, over 103,000 thousand wounded on the field of battle; and untold thousands listed as Missing in Action, let there be no doubt: You went to war. And although victory has never been declared, the purpose was served, and no one knows that better than the people whom you were fighting: the North

Koreans and the Chinese, both under the strong aegis of the Russians.

You, along with the forces from the United Nations, and the troops from South Korea's ROK Army, stopped Communist aggression — and quite possibly World War III, and a nuclear assault that could have crippled the world. It is well over fifty years later; that nuclear threat has largely receded, Communism is but a shadow of itself, and today South Korea — that once disadvantaged country that you defended — is now fruitful, friendly, and free. It is a democracy. But it enjoys that healthy way of life because of what you, the Korean War veteran did in your youth.

It seems like ancient history now, but it also parallels the thought of democracy to recall that not only was Korea a brutal and costly war — with nearly six million Americans serving in the military during the period — it was America's first war wherein there was full integration in the ranks, disproving the altogether spurious notion that when it comes to serving the high ideals of this country there is a difference when it comes to the shade of the skin. In combat, you stood as Americans — shoulder to shoulder. You defended this nation's ideals without fanfare or expectations. You returned home — scarred in many ways, not understanding many things, but even to this day you know the world is a better place because of your sacrifice — and that of many women and other nations that were committed to the cause.

You know, too, that, even without the permission of age, you would do it again if called. When liberty is threatened, America will always put its best foot forward.

It is not to deny nor excuse — in any way — our problems here at home — and God knows there are many — but in all of human history there has never been a greater nation than the United States; and, as I alluded to in a speech not too long ago, if anyone has any doubts about this nation's greatness and/or its global impact, let him or her imagine a world without the United States of America.

It is not to glorify war, but on an international scale, it falls largely to our military to see that America's greatness and values are maintained. In Korea it fell to people like a 1st Lt. Henry A. Schenks, my heroic but still unrewarded patrol leader—who, along with others in the squad, went down fighting; and kept on fighting until there was nothing left to give.

And, my fellow veterans, it fell to people like you, the survivors of a war that prevented a catastrophe and saved a country. It was a country that was on the ropes and was going down for the count. You and your compatriots came to the rescue.

Take pride in yourselves, Veterans. It was a job well done.

Thank you.

July 4th, 2002. It is the result of a marvel of a work by the Second Continental Congress, declaring the independence of the 13 colonies. It is America. And it keeps rolling along.

On one coast they celebrated the national birthday by having a hot dog-eating contest on Coney Island; on the opposite coast there was gunfire in the Bradley wing of the Los Angeles International Airport. Thousands and thousands had their travel plans altered, the heightened fear of terrorism altered the minds of millions more.

It is the new America, a jittery America. But like the old America, it keeps rolling along. It has to. Attatched to it are the wheels of justice, carrying the priceless gift of liberty.

June 25, 2002
Mobile, Alabama
KVA Speech

— Now we gather in the shadows of the USS Alabama, a proud old battleship that served her country well during WWII. We are elevated because we are here to dedicate a memorial, honoring those who fought in a war that never reached the accepted status of WWII, but one that was as necessary as any war this nation has ever fought. The Korean War, as unheralded as it was, was fought to ensure freedom. That freedom was endangered fifty years ago, because of North Korea's invasion of South Korea. It was the scourge of Communism at work. And as retarded as that aggression seems today, I ask those of you who are able, to momentarily go back to 1949 and the early 50s. You will recall the prevalence of the word: Communism; you will recall, too, how frequently the word Atomic Bomb was used. For those of you who don't remember, just two of those bombs, used five years earlier—and crude by today's standards—had already destroyed the Japanese cities, Nagasaki and Hiroshima, killing and maiming well over 150,000 people.

By the early 1950s, the United States had more bombs, but then so did a new enemy of ours, the Soviet Union. A former WWII ally, its grand design now was to spread their doctrine of totalitarianism all over the globe. It was Communism vs. Democracy on the world stage, and many of us didn't know it, but we were on the threshold of an insanity that could have imperiled the Universe. It is entirely conceivable that if the bombs that had savaged Japan's two cities had been used, none of us would be here today.

And so, in the hope of stopping Communist aggression, and in the face of a holocaust that could have doomed the world, the United States, rather than act with abandonment and reckless disregard, turned its eyes to the military. It said: Take your ground troops; go and defend freedom.

For slightly over three years, fighting subzero temperatures, facing a determined North

Korean enemy who fought as though life meant nothing to him, and encountering some 700,000 Chinese troops who swarmed across the Yalu River, and for the first time in American military history, causing some of our units to face the humiliation of retreat on foreign soil, America's troops fought a war that was almost obscene in its dimensions.

With no need to recount the horrors or the heroics here, the troops prevailed. They returned home. They returned in silence; and they returned to a chorus of silence.

With most Americans never understanding what took place on those foreign grounds, and some not even caring, it was a two-way silence that, for the most part, has sustained itself to this day.

From a nationalistic view, it can be argued that since North Korea never surrendered, and the war ended in a stalemate, our involvement does not belong in the front ranks of American achievements, thus a certain amount of si-

lence is therefore justified. While that assess-
ment has merit, the better argument holds that
the objective in Korea was achieved. The
United States, in conjunction with the United
Nations and a committed ROK Army, did
what it set out to do. It put out a fire and prevented a holocaust. There was no dropping
of the Atom Bomb, Communism was stopped;
the Soviet Union — the country that under-
wrote the hostilities is, today, an anachronism;
we have had over fifty years of peace in the re-
gion, and North Korea, the country that tried
its best to dominate the Republic of South
Korea, has been mired in problems since the
fighting ceased, the least of which involves a
backward society trying to hold on to a citizenry,
doing everything imaginable to flee a country
and live free and prosperous in the country that
America and the United Nations defended.

Without question, this country and its allies
has every right to be proud of what occurred on
that beleaguered front in South Korea.

We are obliged to not overlook what was occurring on the homefront during the period, as it was a time of deep and pathetic racial divides in this country, and not — by any stretch of the imagination — that all the problems have been fully eliminated, but to her great credit, the nation did not stop to say: You, Mr. Negro, go here and defend freedom. It did not say, You, with the favored skin go there and preserve democracy; it did not say, You, with the accent of a foreigner, go elsewhere to fight for the cause of liberty. It did not say, either, You, with the dress on, return to the kitchen and retain your sense of wartime anonymity. What this nation did say — and it said it clearly, and to all military commands:

See that your ranks are fully integrated. Then it said to the young men and women in service of the country — as it is saying to the young men and women on the frontlines of freedom today, Go, as one. Go and represent the American people.

That was the mandate in the 1950s; no one could have carried out its execution better than those whom we memorialize today.

Sadly though, the world has moved to an even darker chapter than that which was written on the Korean front. Soon there will be other memorials. As proven by September 11th, this promising new century has introduced us to an age of unparalleled cowardice and evil, helmed by a depraved group whose first series of shots at the bow stunned the world. It is a new Genie, let out of a bad bottle. It cannot be returned. It is a different kind of enemy, and the fight is shamefully masked in the never-ending name of religion. But as irreligious, shallow and commercially-driven as these self-righteous merchants of murder think we are; as splintered, corrupt, and morally-bankrupt as they have taken us to be: America will do what America has always done: Defend freedom; triumph in the time of crisis. This nation will continue to serve for the betterment of mankind.

Because of our position in the world, we will always know international strife, and because of our freedom, we will always be battered by senseless turmoil from within, but its aims are noble and it will forever be a beacon of hope and freedom for the oppressed. And while this new venom called terrorism that has invaded our boarders may momentarily disrupt our course, it will never alter our cause. It is that spirit and cause that has guided us since 1776; it is those God-granted qualities that will carry us for as long as there is a United States of America. In Korea, that spirit and cause transfigured itself into an almost 37,000 young Americans dead on the field of battle; over 103,000 wounded, unnumbered thousands still missing in action, and thousands upon thousands more who are off somewhere, some still suffering the ills of war.

If they could, those who sacrificed so much would thank you for assembling here, and they would salute those who were responsible for this occasion; for this wonderful tribute. And if they were not in silence, they would say, the honor is not for us — but for America.

Like those of us who remain from that front in the 50s, they would say how proud they were to have served a great country, and they would join us in saying how gladly they would do it again. Even in these fragile and waning hours of life; even like this old battleship would do — as anyone who has ever been called to duty would say: I'd serve old glory again and again. I'd do it in a heartbeat. Short of service to God, there is no higher honor.

They would close as we all do, by saying, Thank you, Mobile, Alabama. Thank you for remembering. They would say, too, thank you, my fellow veterans. We knew you would remember; we knew you wouldn't let us down.

May God bless you.

Always and forever,
Etched deep in the vault
of memories,
There is a road called home.
Sometimes it rises
Like a distant trumpet.
Where are you? it sounds.
From somewhere you answer,
I'm on my way home.

It is nicely populated with trees. As a child I knew them. But I did not know them well.

The old hometown revisited.

Nostalgia assails the mind, as the roads to the old place become distantly familiar. There is a mixture of feelings and thoughts as the more recognizable things come in and out of view.

Time, the grand judge of the universe, has summoned bits of yesterday to pass in review.

It has been years. Ages, you feel. For no particular reason, first to be noticed is that the hill that used to be so high isn't very steep any longer. And then there is the school. The old school that used to be so austere and massive isn't very large any more. And so it is with the playground, the store, the trestle, the park, the station — that old station that used to tuck that big, gleaming red fire engine in her womb, and, on a day of unbridled excitement, send her screaming and clanking across the tracks and around the corners — it is not the same. Even the church; that old church with the long, curved pews that sat so benevolently beneath the chained hanging lights — the church where, as precise as clockwork, the pastor used to inflame the air of the Sunday morning congregation that sat so piously hopeful for the grace of a far-off God, is not the same; that church is not the same. Nothing is, really.

The hometown streets are no longer wide and endless; the paths are lost in weeds, the creek is not inviting and is no longer a source of joy.

Even up there, those stately-looking houses that loomed up there in a world of detachment; those big, pretentious structures that peered haughtily down from the hill, those sprawling things that sat up there like a posse of grand overseers, where, when one was a child, only the privileged were allowed to bike, they are not the same.

The place belongs to yesterday.

And the conversation of friends gone by,

too, are of yesterday, as are the questions. Like the answers, they don't come easily.

What ever happened to... to... the local hero and the cute girl who used to live around the corner? They, like others you knew, have passed on. Their deaths were premature. Well, then, the boy who was selected as most likely to succeed? He labors long and menially at the local factory. And the...the one who was headed for the big time? Struck out. Then tell me about that well-to-do family? They've fallen behind, they'll never catch up. And the boy with the curly hair who married that new girl who came to town? Bald, with five children. His brother? Married three times; divorced twice; living with some girl from out of town. Oh, and the big-breasted girl who used to put everything on display? She's in the hospital working on her sixth child; in the courts working on her third husband. And what ever happened to the boy who was leaning on the sweet side? Didn't have a masculine bone in his body. Remember him?

Yep. Got wasted in the war — right through the throat, I hear.

And then there are the victims of monotony, the little soldiers of routine.

Life has passed them by.

Then from the shadows steps a forgotten promise. He is weaving. Alcohol has sapped him of his strength and wreaks havoc with his memory. There are others to see, but you must spend time with him. Growing up, you two were inseparable.

Hi'ya doing? he says, absently.

Okay. And you?

Not so good, but I'll catch up. I'm gonna catch up, just wait an' see. I'll beat 'em yet. I'm just a teensy-weensy tipsy right now, but I'll catch up. ...Say, you — you look kinda familiar; I know you?

You should. We were the best of friends.

Th' hell we were. I ain't never had a friend.

You had one.

...Say, you... you ain't...??

Um-hum. I am.

Well I'll be damn!! I didn't know that was you! I been knowin' you since befo' you went off to the Army; since you came back. Then you went away again! How th' hell you been, boy?!

Not too bad. And you?

S'been a little rough on th' ol' boy — but they can't keep th' kid down. Where you been keepin' y'self lately?

Oh, here and there.

Looks like you got it all goin' for you.

Not really.

Where you comin' from?

Just traveling.

Drive in?

No; flew.

Ain'chu 'fraid of flyin'?

No; pretty nice when you get used to it.

You can have that air. I'm stayin' right down here on th' ground. I'm stayin' right down here where God put me. Down here. On. The. Ground. ... So, howz jobs where you at?

Okay, in some places.

Think you can get me one like yours?

It'd be a little rough.

Why, you too good or somethin'?

I wouldn't say that.

I can do anything you do. S'matter a fact, I might be able to do it just a wee bit better'n you...You know what? In thinkin' it over, I don't want the job. I got more important things to do. Yeah, just for that, I ain't even gonna consider takin' the damn job. Take it an' shove it, for all I care. ...Wha'kinda work you doin', anyhow?

It involves traveling.

What kinda place you livin' in?

House.

Yours?

Um-hum.

A house, huh. Y'must be in the chips?

I wouldn't say that.

Whachadoin' here, anyway?

You might say, I wanted to see the country. But I came here to reflect a little.

Ain't nothin' here to reflect. Ain't a damn thing here worth reflectin'. What kinda business you in?

Oh, just business.

Musta cost a lot, huh?

The company pays for it.

What?! Y'mean somebody pays your way to go someplace?

It's not as big as all that.

Th' hell it ain't! Sure wish somebody would send me someplace. Anyplace...Y'must be makin' good money. How much you make a week?

Not that much.

How old is you now?

We're the same age. Remember?

I hope not; so help me, for your sake I hope not. Look at me. Go 'head, take a good look. I'm a thousand years old an' I ain't lived a day. Y'kno what I mean? I mean it's just about over for me. I been livin' a long time. A real long time, an' I ain't done nothin', I ain't seen nothin', I ain't had nothin', an' I ain't gonna get nothin'. Life ain't been good to me, but I'm gonna catch up. Just you wait an' see who ends up on top. *Me!*

Sure you will.

It ain't been as good to me, like it's been with some people, but I'm gonna catch up. Take yourself; I bet you even stayin' at one'a them fancy places. I bet you even got a rug on the floor. Where you stayin' at, anyhow?

Oh, in some little place.

Bet'chu just sayin' that. Y'don't wanna tell me the truth, 'cause you think it's gonna make me feel bad. But it ain't. I ain't gonna feel bad. Wanna know why? 'Cause I'm stayin in one'a them, too. Know what I mean?

I know what you mean.

— Say, homie, can you let me have a couple o'green ones 'til I get straight?

...Sure. — Here you go.

...Y'mean you gonna let me have all'a this?

It's all yours.

Wow! These are bills!! Big bills!! Aw, man!

Hey, I knew you wouldn't let'cha main man down. Now look, cuzz, y'gonna get this back. Every single dollar back, y'hear? An' th' next time you see me I ain't gonna be on th' jug. I swear it. No more drinkin'. No nothin'! I'm gonna be walkin' proud, an' they ain't gonna have no cause to be talkin' 'bout me th' way they doin' now. I'm gonna fool 'em — every last one of 'em. I'm gonna straighten up. I'm gonna be walkin' tall. An' you know what? I might even come to where you at. Get'a fresh start, y'know? Turn over a new leaf. Yeah, I might do that. Ain't a bad idea, huh? Sounds good, don't it?

Sounds good.

I'm gonna run an' get me one more jug... Ooops, I mean I'm gonna run aroun' the corner to think this thing over, then I'm gonna start packin', 'cause it sounds good to me. I'm comin' out to where you at, an' it's gonna be me an' you. Just like it was when we was kids. R'member? Gotta run now — to get me some... some... er... inspiration, 'cause this is gonna be good. You think about it. S'gonna be me an' you, just like it was in th' old days, r'member? Me an' you?

I remember.

Well, it's gonna be just like that. When I get to where you at, we gonna recreate the old days. We gonna do all the things we did when we was kids; like ridin' skateboxes and scooters, shootin' marbles, makin' stilts and slingshots, an' walkin' on tin cans, an' stealin' apples, an' tossin' stones an' pebbles in the river. Stuff like that. Y'got me?

I got you.

Now I'm gonna take this li'l bit o' change you gave me, an' get me a'coupla jugs... I mean, I'm gonna go get me some er... inspiration, an' think this thing over. 'Cause it sounds great to me. Boy o'boy! ...Me 'n' you, homes, together again. We gonna re-create the old days. Now you take care of yourself, hear?

He wobbles away.

For a long while you stand there looking after him as he retreats to the shadows. Nothing about him is the same. As has yours, his hairline has receded. His teeth are gone, and the jawbone has replaced the muscles of the face. There is that protrusion of the abdomen — like the kidneys and liver have hardened into minimal usage. His gait is slow, and his rear end sags to the demands of aging. There is a deepening of the voice, and, as he wanders farther away, an even more pitiful aura envelops him as he, too, has to somehow realize that it is all ebbing away within the confines of a few blocks.

— You've seen everyone you could see, then the day comes to a close in the old hometown. The all new faces of the children with familiar-sounding names do their best to squeeze in the last few moments of play.

There is the lady sitting on the stoop with the uncombed hair, feeling a bit better after promising herself she will give it a brushing — first thing in the morning. There are the pillars of the neighborhood, gradually withdrawing and surrendering their vigil to the young and more curious.

There is a newborn crying, a dog barking, a cat searching an alley, the giggling of another group of youngsters. And then, from an open window on the second floor of the house across the street, there are the sounds of a couple in sharp disagreement. Further down, there is the mournful sound of the bus, making its last run for the day. It is followed by the echo of a speedster, testing a new muffler as it zooms past the pleading of a man as he sends his hands up the dress of a going-to-submit, unwashed woman. And then the one from the hill drives by. With a superior gloat on his face, he observes much but does not wish for its continuance to be obstructed.

Dusk comes; then the edge of night. It sends signals that it is ready for full deployment. It is noted by the arms of the trees, and they seem to bid one farewell. The good-byes are silent, almost confidential. And so it is with the houses. But there is, too, an undeniable message from the tired old buildings. There is a defiance in them. They defy time. They say they have housed me, and have housed many before me. They say they were squalid then, and they shall always be. They say they know the people, and can prove the people's desires by the grand judge. They say that in my eyes they may appear worthy of condemnation, but in the eyes of those residing in them, they are as kingly as any mansion. They say the conditions, and all that you object to, are but the things or offspring of things you knew so well in your youth. They say — go; leave if you will, ponder what you've head, for the words and all that you have seen and heard may seem strong and objectionable, but to you they are not new. They are not even distantly unfamiliar.

— Yesterday has passed in review.

The grand judge moves on.

Whether those who take a separate path are right or wrong, in the long run it really is not for us to say. We can only try for understanding. What is nice about our race, what is wonderful about humankind as a whole is that there will always be people of courage among us; people of fortitude, of conviction and sacrifice; people of grace and goodwill, and those who make us think.

In this race, too, there will always be people who entertain, who make us laugh and cry, and those who push worry away, and say, if only for a little while, come on in, Fun. Make yourself at home.

—from:
Farewell to the Mockingbirds

Index

Index (continued)

Printed in the United States
5496